TURTLES AND TORTOISES

BY JOAN C. HAWXHURST

Endangered
Animals &
Habitats

LUCENT BOOKS, INC.
SAN DIEGO, CALIFORNIA

Library of Congress Cataloging-in-Publication Data

Hawxhurst, Joan C.
    Turtles and tortoises / by Joan C. Hawxhurst
        p. cm. — (Endangered animals and habitats)
Includes bibliographical references and index.
Summary: Discusses turtles and tortoises including their evolution and lifecycle, hunting and poaching, collecting turtles, habitat destruction, and their future.
    ISBN 1-56006-731-4 (hard : alk. paper)
    1. Turtles—Juvenile literature. 2. Endangered species—Juvenile literature. [1. Turtles. 2. Endangered species.] I. Title. II. Series.
    QL666.C5 H187 2001
    597.92—dc21
                                                        00-009320

Contents

Introduction

TURTLES HAVE EXISTED on Earth for millions of years. At the peak of their populations, they roamed the lands and oceans of the world by the millions. Special adaptations, including protective shells, leathery skin, claws or flippers, and breathing mechanisms, have historically enabled turtles to escape all but the most persistent predators and to thrive through extreme changes in climate and habitat. Even with the protection offered by these adaptations, however, turtles have not been able to adapt to the threats posed by human predation and habitat destruction, and over the last few centuries their numbers have been greatly reduced.

Humans, by hunting and poaching turtles for food and medicine, have severely depleted the numbers of turtles in the wild. Turtle collectors have created a huge and lucrative illegal market for live specimens, and rare turtles are valuable enough that poachers are willing to break international laws to gather them. Turtle eggs, shells, leather, and oil are all products that are in demand in various parts of the world. The demand for eggs is a particularly serious threat to breeding turtle populations, with hundreds of thousands of turtles and millions of turtle eggs taken worldwide each year.

Turtles have been further endangered by destruction of their natural habitats as humans drain wetlands and build homes, roads, and businesses on previously undisturbed areas. Coastlines, tidal marshes, and inland swamps and bogs are particularly attractive to many turtle species, and these same places are prime locations for increasing human activity. Without the particular forms of shelter and food found in their natural habitats, many species of turtles cannot survive.

Sea turtle populations in particular have suffered as a result of onshore development and the increased activity around hotels and marinas, which often disturbs previously quiet beach nesting sites. Shallow offshore waters sustain a rich variety of plant and animal food sources, but they also contain chemical runoff from factories and farms as well as floating garbage, boat traffic, and oilspills. Offshore seas are also the preferred location for the commercial fishing industry, which unintentionally snares and kills tens of thousands of sea turtles each year.

Whether they live in the seas or on land, turtles around the world face serious threats to their survival, all of which can be linked to human activity. As the human population grows and consumes even more of the planet's resources, turtle populations suffer. By combining enforcement of

Turtles have existed on Earth for millions of years.

laws designed to protect endangered species with efforts to save turtle habitats and encourage successful breeding, conservationists are trying to find ways that humans and turtles can coexist and flourish.

Whether certain species of turtle will survive the twenty-first century is still an open question since many species are already close to extinction. In the United States, for example, fourteen of the nation's fifty-four turtle species are either threatened or endangered. Naturalist Richard E. Nicholls warns that a cavalier attitude toward disappearing turtle populations could prove disastrous for humans in the future. He writes, "In a sense, turtles provide an early warning system of the troubles we are visiting upon ourselves. As they now suffer from the degradation of the land and waters, so will we eventually suffer as the devastated land ceases to produce, as the life forms we depend upon die out of the waters. Thus, in taking steps to protect turtles, we are acting for our own good as well."[1]

1

The Evolution and Life Cycle of Turtles

TURTLES FIRST APPEARED on Earth about 200 million years ago, before the dinosaurs, at the beginning of the age of reptiles. They evolved from amphibians called cotylosaurs—lizardlike, insect-eating, heavily limbed reptiles with solid roofed skulls and intricate layers of teeth—who were the first creatures to live permanently on the marshy edges between land and sea. The cotylosaurs developed scales and shelled eggs to protect themselves from losing valuable moisture to evaporation due to the dryness of the air, and they thus attained the freedom to move back and forth between water and land.

The first clearly identifiable turtles emerged during the Cretaceous period, about 140 million years ago, when the dinosaurs were becoming extinct. Evidence of turtles during this period has been found in many parts of the world. These first true turtles were marsh dwellers, but when the marshes dried out, the turtles adapted and moved to other habitats, including forests, ponds, rivers, prairies, and deserts. At some point, a number of species of shelled reptiles returned to the seas, coming ashore only to lay their eggs.

Types of turtles

Today, millions of years after their ancestors' first appearance, all of the living species of shelled reptiles are known as turtles, yet the variety of terms used to describe these creatures can be confusing. In England, the word *turtle* is still generally used only to refer to sea turtles. All nonseagoing turtles are termed *tortoises*. In the United States, however, the word *tortoise* is used only to refer to the species that live on land, such as the desert tortoise; all species that either live in freshwater or are seagoing are known as turtles. The term *terrapin* is also used in the United States to describe edible, mostly aquatic, hard-shelled turtles. For the most part, though, people refer to shelled reptiles (both land and sea dwelling) as turtles.

Around the world, there are three types of turtles: aquatic, marine, or terrestrial. The aquatic species live in freshwater, the marine species live in the sea, and the terrestrial species live primarily on land.

Aquatic turtles

Aquatic turtles split their time between freshwater lakes, rivers, and ponds and the surrounding marshes and woodlands. There are forty-six species of freshwater aquatic turtles in the United States and an estimated 136 species throughout the world, on every continent except Australia. The painted turtle, which is the only North American species of aquatic turtle to be found all over the continent, has vivid red and yellow markings and spends hours basking in the sun on logs and rocks. Painters, as they are sometimes called, are particularly hardy creatures. They can swim under ice in the winter and are able to flourish in man-made ponds and reservoirs, even in polluted habitats.

The largest living North American aquatic turtle is the huge alligator snapping turtle, a 200-pound creature that lives at the bottom of southern rivers and lakes, where it wiggles a wormlike tongue to attract fish. One of these monstrous turtles, on exhibit at Chicago's Brookfield Zoo, weighed 249 pounds, and biologists believe that a bigger one is living somewhere at the bottom of one of the rivers draining into the Mississippi.

Marine turtles

Although freshwater aquatic turtles such as the alligator snapping turtle divide their time between land and water, marine turtles spend practically their entire lives under the sea; the females come ashore only once or twice a year to lay eggs. Marine turtles are capable of making long journeys across the seas but prefer to spend most of their time in more shallow waters close to shore, where their primary food sources are found.

There are six species of marine turtles living in the oceans surrounding the United States, and a total of seven species of sea turtles range throughout the world's oceans. These large creatures are agile and quick in the water but slow and clumsy when they come ashore to lay their eggs because their flippers are adapted for swimming, not walking.

The green sea turtle is one type of marine turtle. It is named for the color of its body fat, which is the primary ingredient in green turtle soup, a delicacy in many parts of the world. The green sea turtle is found in all temperate and tropical waters, including those near Central America, the Bahamas, and the United States. It mainly stays near

The painted turtle spends hours basking in the sun on logs and rocks.

the coastline and around islands. The green sea turtle's diet changes over the course of its life. Young green turtles eat a variety of foods, including worms, insects, and small shrimp and squid. When green turtles reach eight to ten inches in length, however, they become vegetarians, and their diet consists only of sea grass and algae.

The largest reptile alive today is the leatherback sea turtle, which regularly grows to be fifteen hundred pounds and may even reach a length of eight feet and a weight of one ton. The leatherback turtle lives in the tropical waters of the Atlantic, Pacific, and Indian Oceans. Unlike other turtle species, it has no hard shell. Instead, a tough layer of skin covers its back. Its diet is almost exclusively jellyfish, and many leatherbacks die each year after mistakenly eating discarded plastic bags that can look like jellyfish.

Terrestrial turtles

Unlike the great sea turtles, the terrestrial species rarely, if ever, go into the water. Instead, they make their homes in a variety of areas. Some, such as small, unassuming box turtles, live in open woodlands on many continents. Others, like giant tortoises, reside on remote tropical islands

Marine turtles, such as the green sea turtle (pictured), prefer to stay close to shore although they are capable of making treks across the seas.

such as the Galápagos in the Pacific Ocean. The desert tortoise, found in the southwest United States, lives in and around a burrow dug in sandy soil which protects the animal from extreme heat.

Nature's great adaptation: the shell

Despite their differences, all turtles—aquatic, marine, and terrestrial—have one unique feature in common: their shell. The shell is a turtle's defining characteristic and one of nature's most marvelous and practical creations. In one elegant package, it offers protection from the elements and from predators as well as support for the animal's muscles and organs.

Turtle shells are composed of two sections, the carapace and the plastron. Some fifty bones, including the spinal column and ribs, are fused together to form the top shell, called the carapace. Since it is attached to the shell, the turtle's spine is fixed and unable to move. Only its neck and tail bones can move. Another eleven bones make up the bottom shell, the plastron. Both sections are composed of two layers: an inner layer of thick plates of bone and an outer layer of raised plates called scutes, which are made out of a semitransparent hornlike substance similar to the scales of a snake or lizard.

The top and bottom shells are joined on each side, covering the turtle completely except for two openings in the front and back. Through these openings the head, legs, and tail of the turtle protrude. The openings provide great freedom of movement yet allow for quick retraction at the first sign of danger. Some shells, like those of the box and mud turtles, have an extra feature, a hinged plastron that allows the turtle to pull its head, legs, and tail inside and shut the shell completely when it is threatened.

Many turtle species, however, are not able to pull themselves completely inside their shells when faced with danger. The common snapping turtle, for example, has such well-developed legs that they no longer fit inside its small plastron. Since snapping turtles cannot hide their vulnerable body parts inside their shells, they must face their enemies head-on and attack with powerful jaws. Other species that have developed alternative defenses include the musk turtle, or stinkpot, which discharges a foul-smelling fluid when threatened, and the soft-shelled turtle that bites or scratches its enemies.

Types of shells

Despite these alternatives, the turtle's shell has been its primary defense for more than 100 million years, and during that time several different variations evolved. Today, three basic types of shells have evolved for sea turtles, land turtles, and soft-shelled turtles.

Sea turtles found the bulky heavy shell of the early land turtles to be too heavy for swimming in the ocean. As a result, some species traded the horny outer layer for a smooth layer of tough skin. Other species kept the hornlike scutes but in a lighter form.

The land turtles also shed some of the bulk of their ancestors' heavy shells for easier movement. Although they have become thinner, the shells of some land turtles have also expanded. The desert tortoise, for instance, uses the extra space at the top of its higher shell to store water.

The third type of shell variation is that of the soft-shelled turtle, which has discarded the hard scutes in favor of a light yet tough skin over its bones. Such soft-shelled turtles are somewhat misnamed, however, for underneath this skin are the same hard bony plates that protect other turtles. Such turtles also have very flat shells with thin, pliable edges.

The Florida soft-shelled turtle, for example, has a low, round, flattened body, covered by tough skin, and a long neck with an elongated snout. Its flat, soft body provides camouflage when it settles itself into the sand or silt on the bottom of shallow ponds, ditches, and streams. Such an adaptation enables the Florida soft-shelled turtle to hide and breathe without moving or being seen and gives it an advantage over the fish, frogs, crayfish, snails, and aquatic insects that are its prey.

Other special adaptations

Their shells are their defining feature, but turtles also share several other common characteristics. Their necks, for instance, are specially adapted with flexible muscles and extra vertebrae to allow them to emerge from and re-

tract into their shells. Their skin is tough, leathery, scaly, and covered with many wrinkles and folds, which allow for movement of the head, limbs, and tail. Their heads are protected with a layer of thick skin, and their tails are covered with two layers of hard skin.

Turtles have also developed a variety of styles of limbs, depending on their preferred habitat. The nails of the land turtle's feet are actually hardened extensions of its skin and are used for digging, shredding food, and climbing. These adaptations, however, do not allow land turtles to move very quickly, a fact that makes them vulnerable to human predators. One bog turtle, for example, traveled fifty-six feet in a day and took two weeks to cross a meadow six hundred feet wide.

Sea turtles, on the other hand, gradually traded their clawed feet for flippers that allowed them to move quickly in water. The flippers of the sea turtle have no toes and generally no claws, leaving their surfaces smooth and unbroken for powerful strokes through the water. Sea turtles today are capable of attaining the greatest swimming speeds of any living reptile. The Atlantic leatherback turtle, for example, can swim as far as 100 meters (or approximately 328 feet) in ten seconds.

Finally, freshwater turtles combine characteristics of their terrestrial and marine cousins. They have webbed feet for speed in swimming along with clawed toes for walking underwater and on land.

How turtles breathe

The mobility provided by their limbs and the protection provided by their shells have led turtles to develop another unique characteristic: their method of breathing. Since their shells are generally hard, turtles' bodies cannot expand and contract in the same way that mammals' do. As a result, turtles have developed muscles that help force air in and out of their bodies.

Freshwater and sea turtles can also take oxygen from water much the same way that fish absorb oxygen through their gills. The turtles draw water in through their nasal passages and isolate and absorb the oxygen dissolved in the water in their mouths. After taking the oxygen out of the water, the turtle then expells the water out through its mouth. Soft-shelled turtles also absorb oxygen through their skin.

Using these various methods of breathing, turtles are able to remain underwater for long periods without breathing air. Some species can survive on as little as one breath every two hours, and it is not impossible for turtles to spend days underwater without surfacing to breathe. This characteristic makes it possible for many species of turtle to withdraw and hide from enemies for long periods. By avoiding their enemies, turtles are able to live long, quiet lives.

Life cycle

Many turtles live longer than human beings. The eastern box turtle can live to be 120 years old, and other land turtles are reported to live for more than 150, and perhaps even 200, years. Although researchers cannot pinpoint most turtles' exact ages, they believe the animals often live to be at least 50, and sometimes even as many as 70, years old.

The turtle's long life cycle is actually one of the reasons many species are in danger of extinction today. It is difficult for their slow rates of natural reproduction to keep up with the large numbers of turtles being taken from the wild. For example, wood turtles do not mature and begin to produce eggs until they are around fifteen years old. Sea turtles take from ten to fifty years to mature and reproduce. Most female turtles need to live for fifty years to produce a handful of offspring that will survive to reproductive age. Michael Klemens, program director at the Bronx Zoo, explains: "Animals programmed by nature to reproduce for 60 or 70 years are now living for a fraction of that time. They're being taken from the wild or killed by cars and predators like raccoons, which thrive in disturbed habitats. . . . I can look at a population and tell that it's dying out because there are basically no young or teenage turtles, just aging adults."[2] With the disappearance of the younger turtles, the possibilities for turtle populations to sustain themselves by reproducing disappear as well.

Eggs

All turtles reproduce by laying eggs. Female turtles seek out a suitable location and dig a nest in the ground. Depending on the species, the nest may be dug in sand, soil, or decaying leaves. In some species, the turtle uses her feet to arrange the eggs as they are laid. Other turtles allow the eggs to fall unguided into the nest. After all of the eggs are in place, the turtle's hind feet push soil or sand into the nest until the hole has been filled in and the nest disguised. After her eggs are laid and safely covered, the female turtle leaves the area.

Laying eggs makes female turtles vulnerable to predators and is particularly dangerous for the sea turtle. Accustomed to spending all but the earliest moments of her life underwater, her flippers are much more suited to swimming than to crawling across a sandy beach. Yet she drags herself out of the water to dig a nest in the sand and lay her eggs. While she is on land, exposed and slow, she is an easy target for people and animals, so she comes ashore at night in an attempt to avoid detection.

The task of digging a nest may take a female sea turtle more than an hour to accomplish. The turtle—often weighing several hundred pounds—digs a nest cavity with her rear flippers. She then deposits about one hundred pliable Ping-Pong

Turtle hatchlings spend the first years of their lives hiding from predators.

ball-size eggs into the hole, covers them with sand, and returns to the sea.

The larger the turtle, the more eggs she lays. While a female sea turtle might lay up to two hundred eggs, a wood turtle typically lays eight to twelve, and a bog turtle generally lays only between three and five. Few of these eggs will survive to become young turtles. Because the mother leaves her nest behind, the eggs are vulnerable to weather and predators.

Hatchlings

Some of the eggs do hatch, however. After a two- to three-month incubation period, the tiny hatchling turtles emerge from the nest. Usually all of the hatchlings emerge at roughly the same time and scurry off to disappear into the sea or the forest floor. They hurry away because they are defenseless—their shells are soft, and they are small enough to be easily eaten by a host of predators, including raccoons, skunks, and hawks, who swoop down to pluck them from the sand. Scientists estimate, for example, that only one sea turtle hatchling in one thousand to ten thousand will survive to adulthood.

The hatchlings that manage to escape do an effective disappearing act, and little is known about the first few years of life of young turtles. Scientists suppose that hatchling sea turtles hide in great sargassum seas, or enormous clusters of floating seaweed, and young wood turtles are thought to spend their early years in the marshy borders of ponds, streams, and lakes.

Although scientists must speculate about the beginning of the turtle's life cycle, there is one worrisome fact that they know for certain. Around the globe, turtle populations are shrinking at unprecedented rates. Even with their magnificent shells and the other adaptations, even with their long life spans and their variety of different habitats, turtles today face endangerment and possible extinction.

2

Hunting and Poaching

WORLDWIDE, TURTLE POPULATIONS are facing numerous threats to their survival. About half of the world's turtle species face possible extinction, and one of the biggest reasons for this precarious situation is hunting. In most parts of the world, so many turtles are being hunted and taken from the wild that local populations cannot replenish themselves.

Although turtles' shells protect them from all but the most persistent animal predators, shells do not offer much protection against the ingenuity of human hunters. In general, turtles are not equipped for a speedy escape, so they can be caught easily. Sea turtle hunters catch their prey in the water with nets or nooses or overtake and kill the females when they lumber ashore to lay eggs. Terrestrial turtles are usually slow enough to be netted or captured by hand.

Why hunt turtles?

Human turtle hunters have many reasons for catching these animals. Some hunters, especially in subsistence economies, use turtle meat as an important food source for themselves and their families. In other parts of the world, the income derived from selling sea turtle meat, shells, leather, and eggs is a big part of the household budget of poor coastal families. Since turtle is considered by some to be a delicacy, other hunters make a living by selling the meat and eggs to high-end consumers. Hunters also make money by selling turtle shells and skins and by delivering live turtles to exotic animal collectors.

Hunting in all of its forms has dramatically affected the world's turtle populations. Scientists believe that the population of sea turtles, for example, has been reduced by half since the 1970s, mostly because of hunting. Some experts believe that hunting, if not stopped, will lead to extinction for many of the world's turtle populations.

The breadth and scope of turtle hunting is evidence of the high value placed on turtles and their eggs. In fact, turtles have been highly valued since ancient times. Most ancient cultures included images of turtles in their religion, art, and folklore, and many used turtle shells as decorations and as tools. In China, for instance, turtle shells were burned and then examined for divine messages. The Mayans created bowls and containers in the shape of turtles and carved turtles into their temples. Many Native American tribes included the turtle in their creation myths, usually as the wise leader of the animal kingdom or as the foundation on which the world was formed.

In the last several centuries, however, turtles have been valued less for their religious or historical significance and more for the practical uses of their body parts. As humans discovered that certain species of turtle were relatively easy to catch, turtle populations began to be depleted by hunting.

The history of turtle hunting

The first large-scale slaughter of turtles involved the giant land tortoises, which were once found on every continent except Australia. From the 1500s through the 1700s, whaling and sealing vessels traveled extensively across the Pacific and Indian Oceans. As visiting seamen explored various islands along the way, they came in contact with the slow-moving turtles. Discovering that giant tortoises were plentiful, easy to catch, and good tasting, the whalers and sealers captured and slaughtered millions of them. An English pirate wrote in 1684 that the tortoises were "so extraordinarily large and fat, and so sweet, that no pullet [chicken] eats [tastes] more pleasantly."[3]

The slaughter of giant tortoises accelerated when sailors realized that the animals could be taken aboard ship and kept alive for several months without food or water, until the crew was ready to eat them. Typically, several tortoises were killed and butchered while still on the islands, and several more were brought aboard live. The giant tortoises were killed for their meat and for the oil that could be made from their fat. Although there are no exact numbers, many researchers agree that several million, perhaps even 10 million, land tortoises were killed by humans during the last four hundred years. As a result of this overhunting, the once-plentiful giant land tortoises are now extinct in many places.

Hunting the diamondback terrapin

Overhunting also severely depleted populations of the diamondback terrapin in the 1700s and 1800s. Terrapins, with shells that can reach lengths of up to two feet, are similar in shape to sea turtles but have large columnlike webbed feet with claws, not flippers. The diamondback terrapin lives in the marshy fringes of America's Atlantic Ocean coastline, where the land, freshwater, and saltwater come together.

The meat of the diamondback is particularly tasty, and the turtle was hunted almost to extinction because of its

The diamondback terrapin was hunted almost to extinction because of the demand for its meat.

popularity. Found in the sixteenth and seventeenth centuries from Cape Cod to Florida, the diamondback terrapin was a common source of meat for Native Americans and early European colonists. It was so easy to catch—and therefore inexpensive—that it was used in Virginia as a dietary staple for slaves in the 1700s. In fact, there are historical records of slaves protesting over their unending diet of turtle meat.

By the end of the nineteenth century, however, attitudes and supplies had changed, and the meat of the diamondback terrapin became a delicacy reserved for the rich. In the late 1800s, dishes containing the meat of this turtle had become so popular at the most elegant hotels and restaurants that close to ninety thousand pounds of terrapin were caught in the Maryland/Virginia Chesapeake Bay region in 1891. The turtles were sold by the dozen with prices ranging from ninety to one hundred and twenty dollars, depending on the size. At that time, terrapins were the most expensive turtles in the world.

As the terrapin populations were overhunted, fewer and fewer of the turtles could be found at the edges of coastal marshes. By 1920 the Chesapeake Bay harvest was just eight hundred pounds of terrapin, in a region where it had once been plentiful. Gourmet chefs found replacements for the too-rare meat of the terrapin, and demand soon plummeted. Today, the diamondback terrapin is no longer widely hunted, and its population has recovered somewhat from the overhunting of the early twentieth century.

Even though the diamondback terrapin has fallen from favor as a food for humans, many other turtle species are still widely hunted for their meat. For about half of the total number of threatened turtle species, hunting for human consumption is the largest threat to their survival. Wealthy people eat turtle meat as a luxury food, especially in Southeast Asia. In fact, some experts are calling the recent explosion in Chinese demand for turtle products the biggest threat today to the survival of the world's turtles.

Hunting turtles in Southeast Asia

The burgeoning Southeast Asian turtle trade is driven by a huge and increasing demand from China. Long-held

Chinese traditions of eating turtles and using them for medicines are still in existence today. Each year, more than 10 million turtles are imported by southern China from other countries in the Southeast Asian region. Even though turtle species found in Southeast Asia are valuable, some of the most desired species sell for as much as one thousand dollars in Southeast Asian food markets. People purchase these turtles for both their meat and their shells, which are ground into powder for herbal medicines.

This demand for turtles has sharply reduced the region's turtle populations. Many of China's own turtles are pretty much wiped out and several Chinese species only discovered in the 1980s and 1990s are already on the verge of extinction. The three-striped box turtle, for example, once commonly found in Laos, Vietnam, and southeastern China, has been hunted enough that it is now rare, and Swinhoe's soft-shell, the largest freshwater turtle in the world, has been so hunted that experts predict it will soon be extinct.

China's turtle market just keeps growing, and to meet the increasing demand, the nearby countries of Vietnam, Bangladesh, and Indonesia are exporting large numbers of turtles to China. The ripple effect of the Chinese demand for turtles has even reached North America: Many of the more than 7 million turtles of several different species exported every year from the United States, as food or as pets for collectors, end up in China.

Florida soft-shells, for instance, are being caught and sold in great numbers to the large Asian market for turtle meat and bone. This species, which cannot rely on its leathery carapace to protect it from animal predators or from humans, hides at the bottom of streams and ditches, where it is easily discovered by human turtle hunters. Since they are not considered to be endangered or threatened, soft-shell turtles are not protected by law in Florida, and there is no limit to the number of turtles that can be caught or eggs that can be collected.

Turtle meat as gourmet fare

Although it is the largest consumer of turtle products, China is not the only country where the meat of certain turtle species is thought to be a gourmet delicacy. For example, international gourmet chefs prize the meat of the adult green sea turtle, found in all temperate and tropical waters of the world, and consider its meat the best tasting of any sea turtle's. The green turtle grows to weigh up to three hundred pounds, and its body fat is used, along with turtle cartilage, to make green turtle soup.

Some turtles such as this endangered sea turtle are hunted because their meat is considered a gourmet delicacy.

Terrestrial turtles are prized by gourmets for their meat as well. The meat of the gopher tortoise was a staple of some Florida diets long before the now-threatened species was protected by national laws, a fact that did not change after the laws were passed. Despite the fact that hunting this species is now illegal, poachers continue to seek out the gopher tortoise to meet the demand for its meat. In 1998 a Florida man was charged with killing fifteen gopher tortoises after police found tortoise meat in his freezer. His crime was punishable by up to five hundred dollars in fines and sixty days in jail. According to Florida wildlife officials, gopher tortoises are, with the exception of alligators, poached more often than any other protected species in the state.

Sea turtle hunting for food and income

Gourmets seeking exotic game are not the only people hunting turtles for food. People who live in poor countries sometimes depend on turtles as a source of food and income. Sea turtles, the type of turtle most commonly hunted for food, face near extinction as a result of overhunting in these areas. Before the 1960s most coastal people harvested only enough sea turtle eggs and meat to feed their families. In places like Madagascar and Mexico, poor people ate turtle meat because it was one of the few protein-rich food sources they could find or afford. Even today, in many poorer parts of the world, coastal people rely on turtle meat and eggs as a major source of protein in their families' diets, and they conduct small, sustainable harvests. If a handful of hungry locals were the only challenge facing turtles, the animals would be able to withstand some hunting and harvesting of eggs; but in overpopulated areas, even hunting for local consumption can take a heavy toll.

In poor countries, turtle meat and eggs are often eaten by people who depend on the food for protein.

Furthermore, as locals began to realize that they could make money selling sea turtles and their eggs, many started relying on turtle hunting as a source of income. In Mexico, the coastal town of Mazuntle was founded in the 1970s to support the sea turtle slaughtering business. By 1989, when turtle slaughtering was at its highest point, an estimated thirty-five thousand olive ridley turtles were butchered in that area. International attention on this widespread killing of turtles (the entire nation slaughtered nearly seventy-five thousand annually) helped encourage Mexico's president Carlos Salinas de Gortari to outlaw the capture, slaughter, or sale of sea turtles or their eggs in Mexico in 1990.

The plight of the Kemp's ridley

Similarly, the Kemp's ridley turtle, the smallest of the sea turtles at only twenty-four to twenty-eight inches long, has also faced exploitation. Once abundant in the Gulf of Mexico, the Kemp's ridley is an easy species for turtle hunters to exploit for two reasons: It is the only sea turtle species to come ashore to nest during daylight hours, and the females flock out of the surf together to nest on a single beach.

The Kemp's ridley was named for Richard Kemp, who helped discover these turtles, and for the "riddle" of where they nested. The riddle was solved in 1947, when an engineer flying over Mexico's Gulf Coast filmed an estimated forty thousand females laying eggs on a single beach near the town of Rancho Nuevo. The film also showed local people gathering the eggs as fast as the turtles were laying them.

Largely because of overharvesting of their eggs, by the 1970s there were only a few hundred Kemp's ridleys left in the Gulf of Mexico. And in 1998 only thirteen Kemp's ridley nests were found in the entire United States, all on south Texas beaches.

Turtle eggs as aphrodisiacs

Another reason sea turtle eggs are so eagerly harvested is because they are prized by Latin Americans and many others who believe that the eggs are aphrodisiacs, or sex enhancers. Despite laws against collecting or selling them, raw turtle eggs are sold as snacks in Mexican bars for two dollars a dozen. For many of the *hueveros,* or egg collectors, there is no other way for them to make money. According to one local fisherman, "The situation is critical here [in Mexico]. People don't steal the turtle eggs because they enjoy doing it, but because they need to. The people here don't have work, they don't have anything."[4]

The harvesting of turtle eggs happens in the United States as well. Every year a few people are arrested in Florida for poaching endangered sea turtle eggs. In the United States, the eggs are pickled and sold illegally as aphrodisiacs for up to $10 each. In 1999 the owner and the shift manager of a Miami restaurant faced felony charges for destroying the eggs of threatened loggerhead sea turtles. The owner and manager of the restaurant were arrested after an undercover officer purchased six eggs for $1.50 each.

Another way that people—rich and poor alike—make an income from sea turtles is by collecting and selling valuable body parts. Green turtles, for example, are stuffed and sold to tourists as souvenirs. Pacific ridley turtle oil is used in skin lotions and boat caulk. Pacific and olive ridley turtle skins are used for boots, shoes, handbags, and other accessories. Millions of olive ridleys also have been killed for the small piece of skin from the neck, shoulder, and flippers, which is made into supple leather. The rest of the turtle is discarded or used for pet food, hot dogs, or fertilizer.

Tortoiseshell on the black market

Most of these sea turtle parts are sold on the international black market, an illegal and largely secret buying and selling network. Despite the fact that all species of sea turtle are protected by national and international laws, there continues to be a strong and active black market for their body parts in many countries. Even if they have legal restrictions on the sale of turtle parts, some countries, often ones that rely on income from tourism, do not enforce their own laws. A 1995 examination of the shops in many hotels in Sri Lanka, for instance, revealed that turtle products were widely on sale and that laws prohibiting such sales were virtually never enforced.

The hawksbill turtle, often killed for its ornate shell, is the most tropical of the marine turtles.

The most sought-after body part on the black market is the ornate shell of the hawksbill sea turtle. The hawksbill, the most tropical of the marine turtles, lives around coastal reefs, rocky areas, estuaries, and lagoons of the tropical and sub-tropical Atlantic, Pacific, and Indian Oceans. The hawksbill has a narrow head and jaws shaped like a beak. It gets its food—sponges, anemones, squid, and shrimp—from crevices in coral reefs. The shell of the hawksbill, commonly known as tortoiseshell, is beautifully colored and is prized for making a variety of decorative objects such as jewelry, combs, eyeglass frames, and knife handles.

Bekko is a Japanese word for the shell of the hawksbill. In Japan, *bekko* has been turned into everything from cabinets to door posts, hand mirrors to cribbage sets. Furthermore, a long-held tradition of carving the black and yellow shells into ceremonial bridal combs, and newer uses as earrings, tie clips, and bowls, has created a large demand for the shells. Until Japan stopped its large-scale importing of hawksbill shells in 1992, the country reportedly imported thirty-one thousand shells a year, at $375 per shell.

Poaching for collectors

In addition to hunting for shells, meat, and eggs, people hunt turtles to sell them as live specimens to exotic animal collectors. A poacher might receive up to ten thousand dollars on the black market for rare live turtles sought by collectors.

North American turtles that are rare but not yet protected by laws, such as wood turtles and spotted turtles are popular among poachers because they bring high prices. One Florida wild animal dealer sold a rare matching pair of wood turtles for $300. Another sold a set of spotted turtles for $125. These two species, along with two others—the Blanding's turtle and the Eastern box turtle—were legally collected by wild animal marketers in New Hampshire until 1996, when it became the last state to make it illegal to catch, keep, or sell these turtles. Today, in spite of laws making such sales illegal, the Blanding's turtle still brings $50 to $60 in the exotic pet market.

Unprotected rare species such as the twelve U.S. varieties of map turtle can be—and frequently are—also legally exported. U.S. Fish and Wildlife Service figures show that the number of live map turtles legally exported for the pet trade, mainly to Germany and Japan, soared from 673 in 1989 to 56,749 in 1994, the last year that adequate records were kept. The actual number, however, is

Wood turtles like this one are popular with poachers because they bring in high prices and are not yet fully protected by laws.

probably much higher. A 1994 report from the Humane Society of the United States suggests that dealers routinely underreport the numbers of turtles they ship by two or three times since they know that overworked customs agents are usually too busy to notice. These busy customs agents also might not notice if endangered map turtles were mixed in among the other map turtle species.

Collecting destroys turtle populations

Many turtle species are suffering as a result of legal and illegal collecting. For example, dealers illegally collect the unassuming bog turtle, North America's smallest turtle, because it is the most sought-after native aquatic turtle. Collectors, who call it the "Cadillac" of turtles, have purchased bog turtles on the U.S. black market for up to fifteen hundred dollars and the species has fetched up to two thousand dollars a pair in Japan. After it was listed as a threatened species by the U.S. government in 1997, the bog turtle's black market price doubled.

This boom in the bog turtle's popularity has been blamed for wiping out whole populations of the species. As a result, biologists who study bog turtles in the field have become extremely protective and will not reveal the specific sites of their work for fear that poachers will follow them and take the few remaining bog turtles from their shrinking habitats. States do not even share their bog turtle registries with the U.S. government because of fears that this information could be released under the U.S. Freedom of Information Act which gives U.S. citizens access to government documents. So no one person knows the locations of all of the estimated two hundred remaining bog turtle habitats in the United States.

From 1989 to 1994, it is estimated that U.S. collectors paid more than $102,000 for 4,692 bog, spotted, and wood turtles. This is only a small fraction of the world turtle trade, which saw some 25 million live turtles pass through U.S. ports during that time. When combined with the millions of slaughtered turtles, turtle eggs, and turtle body parts being traded as well, the magnitude of the hunting problem is enormous.

3

Fishing and Sea Turtles

ALTHOUGH HUNTING POSES a significant threat to all types of turtles, many environmentalists argue that the largest single threat to the sea turtle's survival is the commercial fishing industry. A comprehensive review done in 1990 by the National Academy of Sciences revealed that accidental capture in shrimp nets accounted for more sea turtle deaths than all other sources of human activities combined. In 1999 alone, according to the Sea Turtle Restoration Project, 150,000 turtles were killed worldwide by the shrimp fishing industry.

Although fishers do not try to catch or hurt sea turtles, their equipment does not discriminate. Shrimp boats, called trawlers, catch shrimp by skimming the bottom of the seas with huge cone-shaped nets, called trawl nets, that scoop up everything in their path. The nets and hooks used by other fishing boats also gather "bycatch," marine animals other than the fish or shrimp they are intended to catch. Worldwide, about 60 billion pounds of bycatch is netted and discarded annually.

Among the marine animals unintentionally snared by fishing nets and hooks each year are thousands of sea turtles, which are often strangled or drowned before they can free themselves or be released when the nets are raised to the surface. Even though sea turtles can remain underwater for long periods of time, they struggle when trapped, thereby reducing their oxygen supply and shortening the time before they need to reach air to breathe. Because shrimp and gill nets are often not removed from the water soon enough to save most trapped turtles, as many as fifty-five thousand adult and juvenile sea turtles, especially loggerheads and Kemp's ridleys, were caught and killed in shrimp nets each year in the waters off the southeastern United States alone.

Turtle excluder devices

The waters of the Gulf of Mexico and Atlantic coast are an important sea turtle habitat, and they are also the main shrimping grounds in the United States. Shrimp is a valuable commodity throughout the world, and in states like Louisiana, Texas, and Mississippi, shrimp fishing is a significant contributor to the local economy, creating jobs and incomes for many people. In Texas alone, 73 million pounds of shrimp were harvested in 1989 and were worth more than $142 million to local commercial fishermen.

So the shrimp fishing industry was understandably concerned when, in response to a U.S. government report indicating that more than ten thousand endangered turtles were being drowned each year in shrimp nets off the coasts of the United States, the Department of Commerce in 1989 ordered all U.S. shrimp trawlers to install special escape devices in their nets. The devices were to be installed during the turtle nesting season, when sea turtles congregate in shallow offshore waters. Shrimp trawlers from North Carolina to Texas were given until the end of 1994 to comply with the new mandate.

The escape device, called a turtle excluder device (TED), is a grid combined with an escape hatch to allow turtles and other large sea animals to slip out of a shrimp net. The shrimp net gradually narrows, guiding turtles to the grid of the TED, through which the smaller shrimp easily pass and continue on into the back of the net. Adult turtles bump against the grid and then slide out to freedom through a weighted hole in the net.

TEDs did make a difference for some turtles in some areas. However, during the 1995 shrimping season, more than four times the usual number of dead sea turtles washed

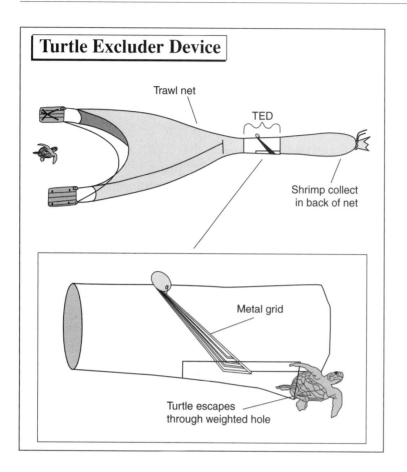

Turtle Excluder Device

Trawl net

TED

Shrimp collect
in back of net

Metal grid

Turtle escapes
through weighted hole

ashore on Georgia beaches, and the government got involved again. A new federal law sought to make the original
TEDs more effective. The 1995 law mandated a change in
the composition of the grid from loose webbing to strong
metal, and the escape hatch was moved from the bottom to
the top of the net. Additionally, the seasonal usage requirement was expanded to mandatory year-round TED usage by
all U.S. shrimp trawlers.

Even with such a strict law in place, dead sea turtles
continue to wash up on U.S. beaches in larger numbers
during the shrimping season than during the rest of the
year. For most environmentalists, the connection is obvious. They claim that some shrimpers are operating without
TEDs and that others sew closed the trapdoor that lets the
turtles escape.

The shrimpers' side

Shrimpers, on the other hand, are frustrated with the requirements, saying they lower the amount of shrimp they are able to catch. Because TEDs can snag on objects on the bottom of the sea or become tangled or torn, shrimpers often lose part or all of their catch. The Texas Shrimp Association, for example, estimates that TEDs and other devices designed to reduce bycatch have caused the loss of 30 percent of the local shrimp catch. Furthermore, the device costs seventy-five to three hundred dollars per shrimp net to purchase and install. The resulting economic impact has led to bankruptcies and shrinking of the Texas offshore shrimp fleet. Fish markets, likewise, argue that the tight restrictions on U.S. shrimpers lead to higher retail prices and importation of lower-quality foreign shrimp.

The shrimpers also contend that the dead sea turtles are not their responsibility. They believe shrimpers are being unfairly blamed for turtle deaths that are actually due to other causes, such as the hunting of turtles and their eggs in Mexico, mutilation by ship propellers, and the effects of offshore oil exploration.

In the hopes of showing the public that turtles are killed by other causes, the Texas Shrimp Association put up twenty thousand dollars of a fifty thousand dollar-reward for the apprehension of anyone caught and convicted of killing sea turtles in Texas. To date, however, the reward has not yielded any publicized results.

TEDs seem to be working

Conservationists say that the inconvenience to shrimpers is a small price to pay to ensure the survival of endangered turtle species. They stand by the laws requiring TEDs, citing a scientific study that found that, for every pound of gulf shrimp that goes to market, ten pounds of bycatch are thrown away. In addition, they are encouraged by the results since the more effective TEDs have been required. In South Carolina alone, the use of TEDs is estimated to have reduced annual loggerhead drownings by 44 percent.

"The turtle population is already coming back," says Scott Nichols of the U.S. National Marine Fisheries Service. "The numbers were down so much in the beginning it was hard even to get experience encountering the turtles."[5]

As a result of those successes, the U.S. Coast Guard has made prosecution of shrimp trawlers without operational TEDs a priority, levying heavy fines. When the owner of one Texas trawler was found to have sewn shut the escape hatch in its net, for example, he was fined ten thousand dollars.

Longline fishing

Once the shrimp industry had been required to make changes in its equipment to protect sea turtles, U.S. environmentalists began looking at problems in other segments of the commercial fishing industry. The first type of fishing equipment they targeted were longlines. In longline fishing, boats trail deepwater fishing lines twenty to seventy miles long with up to two thousand baited hooks, which can accidentally snare sea turtles and other marine life. Longlines are usually set out after sunset, and artificial light is used to attract fish to the bait. Sea turtles, however, are also attracted by the light and can become tangled in the lines or snagged by the hooks.

In the northwestern Atlantic, longline swordfish fleets caught an estimated 1,218 sea turtles between 1989 and 1992. When the Atlantic swordfish stocks were depleted, many swordfish longliners relocated to Hawaii. In Hawaiian waters, where more than one hundred vessels use longlines to target swordfish and tuna, estimates show that hundreds of sea turtles, especially Pacific leatherbacks, are captured by the longline fleet every year. Some survive, but many are strangled by the fishing lines or drown soon after swallowing the hooks. Others die weeks or months later from hook wounds or internal bleeding.

Although longlines have received the most recent attention, other types of indiscriminate fishing are also being targeted by environmentalists. Gill nets, for example, legally used in large numbers off the California coast to catch

Turtles often become entangled in nets used by the commercial fishing industry.

sharks and swordfish, can also snare turtles, and these nets are often not removed from the water quickly enough for the turtles to survive. Similarly, drift nets, which can stretch up to one and a half miles long, are still used in U.S. coastal waters despite a 1992 United Nations ban on them. In the summer of 1998, a small fleet of swordfish boats using drift nets killed thirty-four sea turtles (as well as 253 dolphins and eleven whales) in two weeks of fishing.

No-fishing zones

Environmentalists are calling for the development and requirement of devices, similar to the shrimpers' TEDs, for installation in these other types of fishing nets, but no new laws have been passed. Clearly, despite public attention and advances in some local and national laws, sea turtles still face plenty of danger from the fishing industry. In 1997, 523 sea turtles washed up dead on Texas shores, just four turtles short of the record 527 set in 1994. The number of Kemp's ridley turtles found dead in Texas jumped 40 percent, from 128 to 180. Conservation groups cite these figures when they call for a ban on offshore fishing near the Padre Island National Seashore off the Texas Gulf Coast.

The creation of such permanent no-fishing zones is one idea being considered in the United States and internationally to help save sea turtles. These ocean sanctuaries would be similar to national parks or protected wilderness areas. They would allow stressed populations to rebuild, and they would preserve marine habitat. A few such preserves already exist, in Malaysia and Thailand among other countries, and have had some success but they cover less than 1 percent of the sea surface.

Discarded fishing gear

Even if no-fishing zones were established, latent effects of past fishing would linger. Discarded fishing gear and lines continue to trap and kill marine life all over the world. Sea turtles in particular become entangled when they accidentally swim into discarded lines or attempt to feed on the tiny plants and animals encrusting old gear. When a turtle's neck or flipper gets caught in discarded fishing gear, blood flow is restricted or cut off. Even if the turtle manages to swim away with the gear attached, it may eventually lose its limb or die. Additionally, a turtle trapped in one spot by anchored gear will struggle to free itself, in the process reducing its oxygen supply and shortening the amount of time before it needs to reach air. If the sea turtle is entangled in floating gear and trapped on the surface, it may be hit by a boat or caught by a poacher.

The need for international cooperation

From discarded fishing lines to indiscriminate trawling nets, the threats to sea turtles from the fishing industry are an international problem and require concerted worldwide action. Because sea turtles migrate across the oceans, traveling freely from one country's jurisdiction to another, protective laws enacted by one nation do nothing to protect the animals once they venture into international waters.

With these migratory patterns in mind, the United States is leading international efforts to protect sea turtles from indiscriminate fishing. One attempt, the Inter-American Convention for the Protection and Conservation of Sea Turtles, is an international treaty whose main effect will be

Discarded fishing lines can be lethal to the unwitting sea turtles that swim into them.

the requirement of TEDs in fishing nets throughout the Western Hemisphere. To be effective, the treaty needs to be signed by eight nations. As of May 1999, only Venezuela and Mexico had ratified this treaty. Mexico has been especially cooperative, requiring its offshore shrimp trawlers to use TEDs in Atlantic and Caribbean fishing zones since 1993. But even this regional cooperation will not protect sea turtles who travel from the Americas to Asia and back again since they will still be vulnerable to fishing outside the protected region as well as to egg collectors and poachers who sell turtle meat in Asia.

The United States is also campaigning to extend the use of TEDs to the shrimping industries in other parts of the world. The U.S. Congress expanded the Endangered Species Act (ESA), a law designed to protect endangered animals, to protect sea turtles in U.S. waters as well as throughout their ocean-spanning migrations. The amendment, called the Turtle-Shrimp Amendment, required nations that wish to export wild shrimp to the United States to have laws in place requiring their shrimp fishing fleets to use TEDs. The U.S. law allows shrimp imports only from nations that are certified as having established national policies and practices that require the use of TEDs on all boats.

But the international community has not been widely supportive of this conservation effort. Although Ecuador and Mexico have complied with the U.S. law, other shrimp-exporting nations have been reluctant to mandate the use of TEDs, citing the considerable expense of installing them and the hardship this would cause for their national shrimp industries. Pakistan, Malaysia, Thailand,

and India, for example, recently joined forces to complain that the U.S. ban on imports of shrimp caught without TEDs was a violation of global rules protecting free trade among nations. This anti-TED faction argues that the U.S. law prevents free trade because it places too many restrictions on shrimp imports. The United States, however, disagrees and contends that its law is protected by internationally agreed upon exceptions (for environmental conservation) to the free trade rules.

In 1999, at its meeting in Seattle, Washington, the World Trade Organization (WTO), the global decisionmaker on questions and disputes related to international trade, ruled that the Turtle-Shrimp Amendment was indeed a violation of international free trade rules. The WTO stated that the U.S. law was discriminatory because it provided countries in the Western Hemisphere—mainly in the Caribbean—technical and financial assistance and longer transition periods for their fishermen to start using TEDs but did not give the same advantages to the four Asian countries that filed the complaint.

The WTO's ruling is seen by many observers, from environmental activists to conservative politicians, as an attack on the ESA. This broad and unlikely coalition of

Environmentalists outside the Seattle Convention Center protest the World Trade Organization's rejection of the Turtle-Shrimp Amendment.

people worries that the WTO ruling may lead to cases where an independent nation such as the United States could not exercise its own authority over events within its own borders. Although the WTO ruling does not nullify the U.S. law, if the law is not changed, the United States can face fines or trade sanctions from WTO member nations. Because there can be no further appeal of the WTO decision, the United States and its conservation allies are still considering whether to repeal the law. Since the WTO ruling, no further action has been taken, either by the United States or the global trade organization.

Marketing turtle-safe shrimp

Back in the United States, marketing based on the use of TEDs has turned out to be profitable for some shrimpers. An advertising campaign to sell turtle-safe shrimp on the West Coast has allowed Georgia shrimpers to sell their catch at several dollars a pound above regular market prices. The marketing campaign promises that Georgia shrimpers harmed no turtles in shrimp nets. By looking for the certified turtle-safe label, West Coast consumers know which shrimp was caught using methods that protect turtles.

Georgia shrimpers, like all U.S. shrimpers, are mandated by federal law to use TEDs; they have just found a creative way to use the devices in their favor. More than 125 shrimp trawlers in Georgia have been certified as turtle-safe. Their owners have signed contracts with the Earth Island Institute, a private conservation group sponsoring the campaign, stating that they will comply with all federal and state TED regulations, submit to all state and federal inspections, and allow Earth Island to make surprise checks of their boats.

For sea turtle populations to survive the serious threat posed by the commercial fishing industry, they will need to be the beneficiaries of many more creative conservation programs like the turtle-safe campaign. Until TEDs are used consistently by shrimp trawlers around the world, until no-fishing zones are established to protect nesting females, and until the gear used for fishing, whether still in

use or discarded, is modified to avoid the strangling and drowning of sea turtles, populations will continue to decline. Biologists studying the various sea turtle species declare, "There is ample evidence that human activity is seriously eroding once abundant sea turtle populations. . . . Action is urgently needed to halt the decline and turn the situation around. Otherwise, the extinction of local populations and even some species is inevitable."[6]

Some shrimpers are able to sell turtle-safe shrimp for prices that exceed those of the regular market.

4

Destruction of the Sea Turtle's Habitats

ALTHOUGH HUNTING AND fishing are the most obvious human threats to the survival of endangered turtle species, they are by no means the only ones. Turtles have adapted over many centuries to flourish in almost all types of habitats. Now, in less than a single turtle's life span, many of these habitats are being radically changed or even destroyed by human activity. As human beings bring development and pollution to the lands and seas, turtles often cannot adapt to habitat changes quickly enough to survive them.

Sea turtles, whose migratory habits span the open oceans as well as coastal waters and beaches, are facing habitat threats for a number of reasons. Because of their sheer size and distance from human habitation, ocean waters are regulated and patrolled by law enforcement officials less frequently than other ecosystems. Therefore, damaging activities such as garbage dumping and unethical uses of natural resources also occur more frequently. In the waters where juvenile and adult sea turtles spend most of their lives, pollution, offshore oil drilling, harvesting of great rafts of floating seaweed, increased boat traffic, and construction of artificial sea walls all contribute to the deterioration of the sea turtle's marine habitats.

The sea turtle's oceanfront habitats are being threatened as well. As they become more and more popular as vacation destinations, beaches where sea turtles could easily emerge from the waves to dig nests and lay eggs in the sand are changing dramatically. In many of these previously undisturbed, open areas, there is now increasing tourist traffic, widespread use of artificial lighting, and a wide variety of changes wrought by resort-related construction. All of these changes to the beaches discourage or prevent sea turtles from nesting.

Pollution of the oceans

From ocean beaches where females come to nest to shallow coastlines and deeper ocean waters, unchecked chemical runoff is one of the largest threats to the sea turtle's habitat. Freshwater rivers and streams carrying toxic pesticides and industrial chemicals from farmlands and factories empty into bays and oceans, depositing dangerous toxins that can build up in sea turtles' bodies.

Unchecked chemical runoff endangers female turtles that come to shallow coastlines or ocean beaches to nest.

On both sides of the Atlantic, for example, sea turtles have been found with measurable levels of dangerous toxic chemicals such as DDT and PCBs in their bodies. Scientists suspect that exposure to these chemicals over long periods may weaken the turtles' immune systems and make them more vulnerable to disease. Additionally, such runoff pollution can kill the aquatic plant and animal life that make up sea turtles' food supply.

Another threatening form of pollution for sea turtles is the dumping of garbage into the ocean. Each year thousands of sea turtles die from ingesting or becoming entangled in nonbiodegradable debris floating on the surface of the world's oceans.

Despite international laws prohibiting ocean disposal, tons of debris are still dumped into the sea by ships every day. Sea turtles sometimes mistake the

garbage for food. Floating plastic bags or containers, for example, look like jellyfish, the main source of food for the leatherback turtle. When a turtle swallows plastic, it can suffer in several ways. The plastic can be toxic, leaching dangerous chemicals into the turtle's body. The plastic can also block the turtle's stomach, preventing any food the turtle eats from being digested. In many sea turtles' digestive tracts, biologists have found all types of plastic—bags, sheeting, beads, pellets, line, rope, strapping, pieces of bottles—as well as latex balloons, tar pellets, aluminum, paper, cardboard, styrofoam, rubber, string, cigarette filters, wax, cellophane, fishhooks, charcoal, and glass.

Once dumped into the sea, drifting debris and garbage tends to accumulate in the same floating convergence zones, or areas on the ocean's surface, where wind and waves bring together a semipermanent mass of plankton and algae called sargassum seas or rafts. Hatchlings and young turtles, which scientists believe seek refuge in the sargassum seas, are therefore confronted with especially large amounts of trash in which they can become entangled and die.

There is also mounting evidence that particles from oil and tar spills are building up in the sargassum rafts floating offshore and leading to turtle deaths. Oil on the skin and shell of juveniles and adults can affect breathing and salt gland functions as well as the turtle's blood chemistry, and ingested tar pellets can block a turtle's breathing passages. In one sargassum raft east of Florida, tar was found in the mouth, esophagus, or stomach of 65 out of 103 posthatchling loggerheads.

The mystery of the tumors

According to some scientists, ocean pollution may contribute to another relatively new threat to sea turtles. Fibropapilloma tumors are lobe-shaped tumors that are appearing in rapidly increasing numbers on the bodies of sea turtles around the world. Fibropapillomas can infect all of the soft portions of a turtle's body. They are seen primarily on the skin but can also appear between scales and scutes, in the mouth, on the eyes, and on internal organs.

Many of Florida's green turtles have fibropapillomas on their bodies. The cause of these growths is not yet determined, but scientists suspect that they are a result of a virus that infects the turtles' bodies because their immune systems have been weakened by pollution. Researchers have learned that fibropapillomas are more common in turtles that frequent near-shore waters, areas adjacent to large human populations, and areas with low water turnover, such as lagoons. Because of the nearness of these particular habitats to human activity, their pollution levels are usually higher. Correspondingly, the tumors are less common in turtles that live in deeper, more remote waters. Juvenile turtles seem to be the most affected; fibropapillomas in nesting adults are rare. And so far there is no effective treatment for the disease. Some turtles with fibropapillomas die while others appear to recover and live for many years.

There have been isolated reports of fibropapillomas in turtles since the 1930s, but it was only during the late 1980s that they seemed to reach epidemic levels, specifically among green sea turtles. Researchers recently reported, however, that the tumors are appearing in increasing numbers among other sea turtle populations,

Scientists suspect that pollution is the cause of the fibropapilloma tumors often found on green sea turtles.

and some scientists predict that it will not be long before fibropapilloma tumors become the largest single threat to the survival of sea turtles.

Sargassum harvest

In addition to the threats posed by pollution and debilitating tumors, marine turtle habitats are also being threatened by the harvesting or destruction of the great sargassum rafts that gather in the Gulf Stream and circle the Atlantic. Sargassum is an abundant brown algae that grows near the warm surface waters of the western North Atlantic. Buoyed by air-filled "berries," it floats and travels with the wind and ocean currents. These sargassum rafts offer food and protection to hundreds of species of fish, fungi, invertebrates, sea turtles, and marine birds. Sargassum is particularly important to the survival of hatchling and juvenile sea turtles, which are believed to spend the first year or more of their lives hidden in the drifting sargassum rafts.

Despite its important role in ocean habitats, sargassum is not protected by any national laws or international treaties. During the 1990s, some local Atlantic commercial fishing fleets began to harvest the sargassum as an easy and cheap nutritional additive to livestock feed. In addition, a number of U.S. and foreign companies began to vacuum up the sargassum to make fertilizer, food additives, livestock supplements, and hog medicine. When the algae is vacuumed from the water, however, hidden hatchling sea turtles are also removed. Along the South Carolina coast, for example, "weed lines," the vast stretches of floating sargassum, have vanished in recent years due to vacuuming, and many fewer of the plants wash ashore.

In recognition of the importance of this floating plant in the life cycles of a variety of marine animals, conservation groups have united with the fishing industry in campaigns to stop the removal of sargassum rafts from offshore waters. In 1998 the South Atlantic Fishery Management Council (SAFMC), concerned that the loss of sargassum was leading to lower fish catches, voted to ban the harvest

and possession of sargassum in the South Atlantic effective January 1, 2001. "We don't believe there should be a directed harvest on essential fish habitat,"[7] said Bob Mahood, executive director of SAFMC. But in October 1999, the U.S. National Marine Fisheries Service suggested that regional fishing councils limit, not ban, the amount of sargassum being harvested in their areas. Neither proposal has been passed, however, and the question of how much sargassum can be sustainably harvested is still open for debate.

The destruction of sargassum (pictured) has dire consequences for sea turtles, which depend on the floating algae for food and protection.

Dredging and drilling

Although there is little scientific data to help determine sustainable levels of sargassum harvesting, there is sufficient information to support limits on other types of human activity in coastal waters. The activities involved in offshore oil and gas exploration, for example, have been proven to negatively affect sea turtle habitats. Finding and extracting the undersea oil and gas that humans need to power their cars, industries, and homes require dredging the ocean floor to construct offshore drilling platforms. Dredging and drilling on the ocean floor can destroy or disturb the plants and animals eaten by sea turtles. Later, once the construction of offshore drilling platforms is completed, sea turtles often become comfortable foraging on the plant and animal life that grows on and around the platforms. Then, when the platforms are destroyed, sometimes by underwater explosions, sea turtles can be killed or seriously injured in the process. Scientists estimate that between fifty and five hundred sea turtles are killed by explosive platform removal in the Gulf of Mexico each year.

Sea turtle habitats are also affected by dredging done for other reasons. Workers regularly remove underwater soil from the bottom of shipping and recreational boating channels to keep them deep enough for ships and boats to pass through. Other times, people dredge underwater soil to fill in low-lying coastal lands for development. Both of these types of dredging disturb the plant and animal life on which sea turtles depend for food and sometimes crush and kill turtles that get in the way.

Boat traffic

Dredging boat channels also causes other problems for sea turtles. Deeper channels allow more boat traffic, and increased boat traffic leads to more turtles being injured or killed by moving engine propellers. The problem of propeller strikes is particularly bad during nesting season, when great numbers of sea turtles congregate in the shallow waters just off beaches. Those same shallow waters also tend to be where commercial and pleasure boat traffic is the heaviest. Biologists estimate that countless numbers of loggerheads and five to fifty Kemp's ridley turtles are killed each year by boat traffic in the United States alone. In the early 1990s in Florida, for example, where coastal boating is particularly popular, almost 20 percent of the turtle strandings—when a dead or dying turtle washes up on a beach—had signs of boat propeller injuries.

Increased boat traffic is only one aspect of the increased activity level on and around the ocean coasts. As beaches become popular vacation and retirement destinations, they are rapidly being lined with condominiums, hotels, and private homes. The quiet, undisturbed beaches that sea turtles seek out to lay their eggs are becoming increasingly difficult to find.

Artificial lighting

One of the biggest and most detrimental changes to these beach habitats is the addition of artificial lighting such as streetlights, lighted signs, and the lights in and around waterfront homes, resorts, and hotels. Because it disrupts the natural darkness of nighttime, such artificial lighting can wreak havoc on turtle nesting. Most sea turtles, being slow and clumsy on land, wait for the protection provided by the darkness of night before coming onto the beach to lay their eggs. The bright lights of beachside hotels and boardwalks, however, can deter females from coming ashore for fear of being discovered. Additionally, the females can become disoriented and mistakenly follow the lights inland after laying their eggs.

Even if the female turtle does complete her nest and return safely to the sea, her offspring will face similar dangers. Hatchlings, which emerge from their sandy nests at night,

A turtle lies stranded on a beach. According to a 1990 study, 20 percent of stranded turtles in Florida had signs of boat propeller injuries.

also face the challenge of returning to the sea. Scientists think that these hatchlings have an inborn tendency to move in the brightest direction. Historically, they relied on the natural nighttime sky, as reflected in the ocean, to guide them back to the water. Streetlights, porch lights, illuminated signs, or interior lighting visible from the beach can confuse the hatchlings, causing them to head toward the source of that light instead of returning to the sea. When the hatchlings head away from the sea, they are often crushed by cars or killed by terrestrial predators or heat exhaustion once the sun rises.

Human activity on nesting beaches

In addition to artificial lighting, other human disturbances on ocean beaches—noise and physical barriers, for instance—prevent turtles from successfully nesting. Parties, bonfires, and recreational equipment, such as umbrellas and chairs left on beaches at night, confuse females coming ashore to lay their eggs. Even nighttime turtle-watching expeditions, organized by local sea turtle conservation groups, can occasionally cause enough noise and disruptive activity that

A sign placed in front of a sea turtle nest wards off beachgoers, whose activities often hinder turtle breeding.

female turtles return to the sea without building their nests. These turtles may delay egg laying, coming back to the same beach another night, or they may end up digging a nest on a less suitable but more private beach, where fewer eggs may hatch due to poorer sand quality and temperature differences.

Nighttime is not the only time when the turtle nesting process is threatened by human activity. During the day, heavy vehicles driven on the beach, from jeeps to beach-cleaning equipment, can collapse nests and crush turtle eggs and preemergent hatchlings. And once they emerge from their nests, hatchlings can be caught in the tire ruts resulting from vehicular beach traffic. Loggerhead hatchlings can escape from a one-inch-deep footprint, but they are unable to get out of a tire rut of similar depth because the rut's sides are vertical and difficult to climb. They may crawl along in a rut, even if it takes them away from the water they need to reach.

Erosion control and repair

Although tire ruts are not lasting changes to the structure of the beach and eventually are washed away by the waves or blown away by the wind, some changes to the beach's landscape are more permanent. To protect beach-front development from also being washed or blown away, developers build erosion control structures such as sea walls, bulkheads, or jetties. These structures can significantly change the beach and prevent female turtles from coming ashore to nest. If a turtle cannot climb over a concrete wall or a bulkhead, she cannot get to the sandy beach where she needs to lay her eggs. Such structures can also turn an area of dry sand suitable for nesting into a wet area where turtles will not leave their eggs.

The practice of beach nourishment, in which new sand is brought in to replace sand lost to erosion, can have detrimental effects on nesting as well. The replacement sand is sometimes of a different composition or temperature than the original sand. If the clay, silt, and shell content is too high, the beach becomes too compacted for turtles to dig proper nests. If the replacement sand has a different heat

Changes in beach sand temperature caused by beach nourishment can disrupt the male-to-female ratios of sea turtle hatchlings.

capacity or moisture retention than the original sand, fewer young turtles may survive. In Florida, for example, local sources of replacement sand have been exhausted, and the sand that is being imported from the Bahamas stays slightly cooler than the original beach sand. Since cooler temperatures during incubation cause more male hatchlings to emerge, even this slight temperature change can lead to changes in the male-to-female ratios of hatchling sea turtles, disrupting the natural balance between the sexes.

The threats to sea turtle habitats, including erosion control and repair, artificial lighting, boat traffic, and ocean pollution, become greater as the level and scope of human activity increases around the world. Overnight, actions by humans can throw off the delicate balance created by the natural world. In the oceans and on dry land, turtles are struggling to adapt in a world dominated by humans.

5

Destruction of Land and Freshwater Turtle Habitats

WHETHER CONSCIOUS OR not, the choices humans make when they change the natural world clearly affect turtle habitats and populations. On land, as developers alter previously untouched marshes and woodlands to construct houses, roads, and businesses, the habitats of freshwater and land turtles shrink or disappear, threatening the survival of a number of species. And as large-scale agriculture and industry allow dangerous chemicals to run off into turtle habitats, remaining habitats are polluted and more species are threatened with extinction.

People were changing and affecting the natural habitats of turtles long before the Industrial Revolution opened the door to large-scale agriculture, industry, and development. After Europeans settled on the Pacific and Indian Ocean islands in the 1600s, the giant tortoises they found there became part of their staple diet, and tortoise populations started to decline from overhunting. The island settlers also brought dogs, rats, pigs, and goats—as pets, stowaways, and new sources of meat. These new animals, which were not native to the islands, began to prey on turtle eggs and hatchlings and to compete with the tortoises for food. These new predators thus destroyed the natural ecological balance and further shrank the tortoise population until the giant animals were endangered. Today, the once-abundant giant tortoises exist only on several widely separated islands: Aldabra Island, located in the Indian Ocean off the east coast of Africa, and the Galápagos Islands in the Pacific Ocean.

Development

By far, however, the largest threat to turtle habitats is development. As U.S. cities and suburbs expand to accommodate growing human populations, many of the sites being chosen for development are marshes, bogs, meadows, and woodlands—all important turtle habitats.

For terrestrial turtles, whose complex habitat includes a combination of wetlands and drier forests and meadows suitable for nesting, it is increasingly difficult to find areas that are not razed by new roads and developments. When humans build roads through turtle habitats, many turtles are killed by cars as they try to cross the roads. "A wood turtle might travel two miles from its riparian [riverbank] habitat," says herpetologist Michael Klemens of the Wildlife Conservation Society at the Bronx Zoo, "but there is no population in Connecticut that's less than a mile from a paved road. Every wood turtle in the state crosses a road

The habitat of the endangered Galápagos tortoise was changed when island settlers introduced new predators such as pigs and dogs.

at least once or twice a year, and a lot of them get run over."[8]

Destroying the wetlands

All over the country, these areas are being divided, cleared, and filled to build houses and businesses, in the process destroying, fragmenting, or shrinking habitats. The Illinois Natural History Survey, for instance, reports that only about 10 percent remains of the estimated 9.4 million acres of wetlands that existed in Illinois before European settlement.

Even when wetland areas are left intact, they are often designated as sites for stormwater channeling. The additional thousands of gallons of rainwater, along with whatever chemicals and pollutants they pick up along the way, seriously disturb the delicate balance of life in the wetlands.

When wetland habitats are destroyed or altered, the sensitive Blanding's turtle is often among the first creatures to disappear. This turtle, named for the Philadelphia doctor who discovered it in the early 1800s, prefers shallow marshes and ponds. Once common from Nebraska to Massachusetts, the Blanding's turtle is now on threatened or endangered lists in a number of U.S. states where development has destroyed its wetland habitats.

Draining and filling marshes and ponds is a direct effect of development, but there are indirect effects as well. One of the indirect effects increasing development has on the habitat of the Blanding's turtle is the altered balance between animal species. Human communities bring garbage and landfills, providing new sources of food for growing populations of raccoons, ravens, and foxes, all of whom are natural predators of the Blanding's turtle, and have adapted successfully to life alongside human development. So, as the turtle's habitat is being squeezed smaller and the number of its natural predators is increasing, the Blanding's turtle faces the double threat of decreased habitat and increased predation.

The fate of the bog turtle

The bog turtle, North America's smallest turtle at three to four and a half inches long, has faced similar challenges.

Bog turtles like this one are adversely affected by the fragmentation, filling, or draining of their wetland habitat.

This species, whose habitat includes marshy meadows, swamps, and bogs in eastern states, has been adversely affected as the wetlands are filled, drained, or fragmented. About one-third of the bog turtle's habitat was in the state of Maryland, but much of that has been lost to new suburban homes, shopping malls, and office parks. As the wet meadows where the bog turtle lives have been drained, filled, or surrounded by development over the last twenty-five years, the native population has dropped by half. Researchers estimate that fewer than ten thousand bog turtles are left in the wild, living in about two hundred wetland habitats in seven states from Massachusetts to Maryland. Of these two hundred habitats, fewer than one-fifth are in good condition, the rest having suffered the effects of pollution, stormwater drainage, or nearby development.

In 1997 the U.S. Fish and Wildlife Service (USFWS) listed the bog turtle as a threatened species. In its report, the USFWS stated that three of the eight known bog turtle sites in Connecticut alone have already been ruined by industrial development, pond construction, residential development, and natural plant succession. The bog turtle is, according to *USA Today,* "the first denizen [inhabitant] of the Boston-to-Washington metropolitan corridor to face such a fate, and arguably the first species to be threatened by nothing more or less than suburbanization."[9]

Scientists see the problems facing the bog turtle as indicative of the larger questions surrounding development of natural habitats. "The bog turtle's problems are our problems: loss of watershed, loss of open space," says Michael Klemens. "We can't save the bog turtle without dealing with surburban sprawl. We're not just saving a turtle; we're saving a . . . landscape."[10]

Spreading disease

In addition to the dangers to turtles brought by land development, there are other less obvious ways that humans endanger terrestrial turtle habitats. The rare Florida gopher tortoise, for instance, is being hurt by humans who are trying to help it. Formerly common, the gopher tortoise is listed as endangered in several states and is a "species of special concern" in Florida, where many of its remaining populations are declining; estimates show that the original number of tortoises has decreased by 80 percent over the last one hundred years.

Researchers contend that the Florida gopher tortoise's number is dwindling because a highly contagious disease is being spread among local populations as motorists and

Scientists link the bog turtle's shrinking habitat to suburban sprawl.

developers come into contact with the tortoises. A motorist who stops to help a gopher tortoise make it across the street and then releases the tortoise in a faraway field, for example, may be helping to spread a respiratory disease that has infected 60 to 70 percent of these animals. Since the early 1990s, developers in Florida have been required by law to move gopher tortoise colonies off of land where they plan to build. There is growing concern that turtle colonies moved to make way for development are also spreading the highly contagious upper respiratory tract illness.

By transporting infected tortoises to uninfected areas, people who think they are helping may actually be contributing to the extinction of this species. "In saving one tortoise, you may be killing 1,000," says Ray Ashton, a biologist who runs a private tortoise research site in Florida.

A similar respiratory disease has nearly eradicated the few remaining western desert tortoises as well. Desert tortoises are found in the Mojave Desert of Nevada and California, and they have been endangered by habitat loss, off-road vehicles, and cattle that eat their forage. Adult desert tortoises range

Habitat loss, off-road vehicles, and lack of food endanger the desert tortoise.

from four to thirteen pounds, mature in fifteen to twenty years, and lose water at such a slow rate that they can survive for more than a year without access to water of any kind. The desert tortoise's ability to tolerate large imbalances in its water and energy supply enables it to survive lean years and feast on plants that are only periodically available.

These adaptations allowed the desert tortoise to thrive for many years. Today, however, its populations are threatened by a contagious upper respiratory tract disease. People are advised not to pick up these tortoises and not to release pet tortoises into the wild because such actions can help transmit the disease. In fact, it is a violation of law to release a desert tortoise into the wild.

Destruction of the rain forest

Far away from the desert southwest of the United States, the habitats of other terrestrial turtles are threatened as well, sometimes not for the sake of development but for the raw materials that can be extracted from the habitat. The demand for expensive furniture, for example, starts a chain of events that impacts animal habitats far from the furniture's final destination. In Southeast Asia, for instance, the spiny turtle, which looks like a walking pin cushion, lives in the shallow clear streams and shaded plant debris of mountain rain forests. Its habitat is full of teak and mahogany trees, which are particularly valuable for the expensive furniture made from their wood. Because they are so valuable, teak and mahogany trees are often harvested in great numbers at one time, using a fast but destructive method called clear-cutting.

Such indiscriminate clearing of the rain forests leaves a totally destroyed habitat in its wake. The clumps of grass and plant matter that once concealed and protected the spiny turtle are trampled or bulldozed by the heavy equipment used to harvest the lumber. Frequent heavy rains wash loosened topsoil into streams and rivers, clouding them and killing the animals and plants on which the spiny turtle once fed. With the food and protection offered by its habitat destroyed, the spiny turtle cannot survive.

Pollution on land and in freshwaters

Lumber is not the only material harvested at the expense of turtle habitats. Even harvests of farm-grown fruits and vegetables can threaten turtles' survival. Modern farming methods rely heavily on insecticides and herbicides to produce large harvests of uniform crops. Farmers often overlook the fact that these chemicals, which can be toxic to turtles and other wild animals, are carried by air and rain away from their fields. Likewise, factories that allow chemicals to escape during the manufacturing process also pollute areas much larger than their immediate surroundings. Carried by rain and wind, pollutants end up in soil, streams, and rivers in faraway turtle habitats, where they can linger for many years. Chemicals from industrial and cropland runoff are then stored in terrestrial and freshwater turtles' body fat, and high levels of such dangerous chemicals can later poison a turtle as it fasts (using its fat for energy) when food is scarce.

DDT, for instance, was a commonly used agricultural pesticide until the 1970s, when it was linked to reproductive dysfunctions, such as thin eggshells in some birds and possible human diseases. PCBs, another group of toxic chemicals, were once commonly released during industrial manufacturing. Chemicals like DDT and PCBs, which have been banned in the United States for years because of their dangerous effects on animals and people, still pollute the mud and silt at the bottoms of U.S. lakes and rivers. When snapping turtles hide and dig for food in this contaminated mud, they ingest DDT and PCBs. Snappers from the Great Lakes region and New York's Hudson River valley have been found to have high levels of these deadly chemicals in their bodies. Scientists believe that these chemical pollutants, which enter turtles' bodies both from the mud in which they hide and from the contaminated prey they eat, may be behind the recent decrease in snapping turtle eggs and the increase in deformed snapping turtle hatchlings in these regions.

Furthermore, toxic chemicals are particularly dangerous to turtles with small habitats, such as aquatic map turtles, which are prized by collectors for the beautiful maplike markings on their shells. Map turtles, of which there are twelve species in the United States, are extremely vulnerable to small but concentrated amounts of chemical pollution. Nine of the twelve species have very small ranges, and two species are currently listed as endangered: the ringed map turtle, which is confined to the Pearl River watershed in Mississippi and Louisiana, and the yellow-blotched map turtle, found only near the mouth of Mississippi's Pascagoula River. Such small ranges make these turtles especially vulnerable to pollution; scientists hypothesize that an entire species could be wiped out by a single toxic spill from a nearby factory or by chemical runoff from an overzealous farmer's well-sprayed crops.

Chemical pollution like this can happen quickly and lasts a long time. Once toxic chemicals are spilled, sprayed, or leaked into a local water source, they remain in the water and soil for many, many years. Likewise, a new suburban strip mall built on a drained and filled marsh will have a long-lasting effect on local turtle populations. These threats to turtle habitats, once put in place, cannot easily be undone.

6

The Law and the Future

ABOUT HALF OF the world's turtle species are currently facing the threat of extinction. The crisis facing endangered and threatened turtle species is severe enough that people who understand it are speaking out. The publisher of the *Turtle and Tortoise Newsletter,* Anders G. J. Rhodin, recently sounded a strong warning:

> Turtles are in terrible trouble. Throughout the world they are threatened by a plethora of problems to which they are succumbing. Their habitats are being increasingly fragmented, destroyed, developed, and polluted. They are being collected, butchered, eaten, traded, sold, and exploited in overwhelming numbers. They are used for food, pets, traditional medicine—eggs, juveniles, adults, body parts, all are utilized indiscriminately, with no regard for sustainability. Populations nearly everywhere are shrinking. Species everywhere are threatened and vulnerable, many are critically endangered, others teeter on the very edge of extinction, some have already been lost forever. . . . We are facing a turtle survival crisis unprecedented in its severity and risk. Without intervention, countless species will be lost over the next few decades.[12]

Many people—scientists, legislators, tourists, developers, and environmental activists—have joined together to try to prevent this from happening. Scientists hope to conserve the diversity of turtle species for future study. Legislators want to protect species that live within their districts. Tourists and resort developers both want turtles to remain part of their vacation experiences. And conservationists and environmental activists hope to protect the natural environment so that it can be enjoyed and explored by future generations.

People are working to prevent the extinction of turtles in two basic ways: the enactment and enforcement of laws and treaties prohibiting activities that endanger turtles and conservation efforts aimed at helping turtles breed and flourish. Legislation aimed at protecting turtle populations—whether by prohibiting hunting and collecting, by preventing entrapment in fishing nets, or by protecting habitats—has been passed at the local, national, and international level. Tough, protective laws are in place, but enforcement remains an issue at all levels of government.

The Endangered Species Act

In the United States, the centerpiece of the legislative effort to protect endangered species such as turtles is the Endangered Species Act (ESA) of 1973. When President Richard Nixon signed this bill into law, he stated, "Nothing is more priceless and more worthy of preservation than the rich array of animal life with which our country has been blessed."[13] The purpose of the ESA is to preserve the nation's natural heritage for the enjoyment of current and future generations by offering protection to species that have been accepted for inclusion on its two lists. A species is included on the endangered list if it is in danger of extinction throughout all or a large portion of its natural habitat. A species is on the threatened list if it is likely to become an endangered species within the foreseeable future.

The ESA protects several species of marine, aquatic, and terrestrial turtles, making it illegal to harm, harass, or kill adult turtles, hatchlings, or their eggs. It is also illegal to import, sell, or transport these turtles or their byproducts. Under the ESA, fines of up to fifty thousand dollars and prison terms have been set in place for people caught selling, exporting, or importing threatened or endangered turtle species.

Generally, the U.S. Fish and Wildlife Service coordinates ESA activities for terrestrial and freshwater species while the National Marine Fisheries Service (NMFS) is responsible for marine species. Both of these national agencies are charged with conserving and protecting wildlife, plants, and habitats for the continuing benefit of the American people. They conserve and restore wildlife habitat such as wetlands and beaches and help foreign governments with their conservation efforts.

In 1998 the NMFS added to the protective power of the ESA by setting up a Protected Resource Enforcement Team. This team travels to areas where endangered and threatened sea species are found dead to investigate why the animals are dying. The first deployment of the enforcement team was to Padre Island National Seashore in Texas, where record numbers of dead sea turtles washed ashore in early 1998. The team boarded shrimp boats to check their TEDs and looked for other possible causes of the turtle deaths.

They found several. In one instance, they rescued a drowning loggerhead turtle from a shrimper's net. The team also found a number of shrimp boats with their TEDs illegally sewn shut. In these cases, the NMFS levied fines

Stuffed turtles are displayed in front of a Balinese store. The Endangered Species Act and other laws have been passed to protect endangered turtles from a similar fate.

and confiscated shrimp catches to penalize the owners of these boats.

States have added to the power of the ESA by passing their own species protection laws. The state of Florida, for example, has passed the Marine Turtle Protection Act, giving state agencies the power to enforce regulations protecting turtles and their habitat. Other local coastal governments have passed regulations to eliminate or control artificial beachfront lighting. And many states have passed laws aimed at preventing the poaching of rare turtle species.

International efforts

In an effort to reduce the killing of turtles, national and international bodies have also enacted laws making it illegal to hunt certain turtle species, especially sea turtles. From Mexico to India, countries have responded to plummeting turtle populations by enacting laws limiting or prohibiting the hunting of turtles and their eggs. In May 1990, for instance, the government of Mexico passed a law prohibiting the killing of sea turtles in Mexican waters or on Mexican beaches and setting aside special nesting areas.

The effects of the Mexican law were almost immediate. Researchers estimate that the number of sea turtle nests on one Mexican beach, the destination for olive ridley turtles who typically congregate in large numbers to lay their eggs all on one night, increased from about sixty thousand in 1988 to more than seven hundred thousand in 1995.

But even when clearly worded and reasonably enforced national laws such as these are in place, illegal turtle hunting remains a problem in some places. On Mexican beaches, for example, where six of the seven species of sea turtles go to nest, hungry people ignore strict laws against harvesting turtle meat and eggs. With few economic alternatives, these people continue to feed themselves and their families with the meat and sell the turtle eggs and skin.

CITES

Such small-scale subsistence hunting of turtles, however, is not the primary concern of global lawmakers, who focus instead on the international trade in turtles and turtle parts. Worldwide there are more than seventy international conservation laws and regulations that apply to turtles. The most important is the Convention on International Trade in Endangered Species of Wild Fauna and Flora (CITES), which grew out of an international meeting of concerned nations in 1975. Recognizing that the survival of a species on one continent may be linked to demand for it on another, CITES controls and regulates global trade in wild animals and plants that are or may become threatened with extinction because of commercial trade. Currently 146 nations, including the United States, belong to CITES. Members meet about every two years to discuss improvements to the treaty and to review protections for wildlife.

CITES offers three levels of protection. Species listed in Appendix I are the rarest and may not be bought or sold commercially anywhere in the world. Species listed in Appendix II are threatened and may be bought or sold only with special export permits that are carefully regulated. Species listed in Appendix III may someday be threatened, and their purchase or sale is also regulated by special permits. CITES currently protects all species of sea turtles and many species of terrestrial and aquatic turtles.

In April 2000, CITES delegates from around the world met in Nairobi, Kenya, to update the appendix listings. At this meeting, the U.S. delegation proposed that several additional turtle species be added to the CITES lists. The spotted turtle, for example, is threatened, both in the U.S. and internationally, by over collection and habitat destruction. The proposal to include this species in Appendix II, however, was rejected by a close vote. Nine species of Southeast Asian box turtles, on the other hand, were listed in Appendix II due to their heavy use as food throughout their native region. And the rare pancake tortoise, native to Kenya and Tanzania, was proposed for Appendix I.

The proposal to add the threatened spotted turtle (pictured) to Appendix II, a list of species whose trade is regulated, was denied at a recent CITES meeting.

CITES is the most influential international agreement, but there are other international conservation laws and regulations that apply to turtles. The Convention of Migratory Species of Wild Animals, for example, addresses endangered species that migrate from one governmental jurisdiction to another, like sea turtles, on the premise that it does little good for one country to enact and enforce protective laws if its neighbors, or even countries across the ocean, allow hunting of a species that travels back and forth. And another effort, the International Convention for the Prevention of Pollution from Ships (commonly known as the MARPOL treaty), aims to protect marine animals such as sea turtles by making it illegal for any vessel to dump plastic trash anywhere in the ocean.

A lack of global enforcement

However, no number of laws will provide protection unless they are enforced. In many countries, CITES listings and other treaty agreements are ignored or not understood by customs and conservation officials. A lack of enforcement of existing trade regulations is seen by many experts as one of the most critical threats to turtles' survival. In China and other parts of Southeast Asia, for example, there is very little governmental monitoring of the turtle trade and little regard is paid to whether the turtles being traded are listed by CITES. In these areas, endangered species are caught and sold alongside the more common species. Furthermore, it is sometimes difficult to identify an endangered or threatened species of turtle, and with limited resources dedicated to trade agreement enforcement, such species often slip by unnoticed.

To address the critical problem of identifying endangered and protected species, the Chelonian Research Foundation, an American conservation group, suggests that turtles need to be more broadly protected. According to Anders G. J. Rhodin, "Perhaps we need to begin thinking about possibly listing all [turtles] on at least CITES Appendix II, as are many other whole groups of traded animals. All marine turtles and all tortoises are already listed by CITES; it may be time to list all freshwater turtles as well, thereby providing at least some degree of monitoring for all [turtles] in international trade."[14]

Tortoiseshell trade

Even though the Southeast Asian demand for turtle meat continues to be strong in defiance of international protective treaties, global demands for other turtle products have lessened. Largely because of worldwide publicity about the plight of sea turtles, the huge trade in tortoiseshell has dropped off somewhat in recent years. In 1992 Japan agreed to ban imports of tortoiseshell until a sustainable supply of the shell could be obtained that did not compromise the conservation of wild hawksbill turtles. Since hawksbill turtles are frequently, although accidentally, caught in legal fishing operations around the world, stockpiles of tortoiseshell are accumulating in many countries that used to export these shells to Japan.

In 1998 the government of the Seychelles made a public spectacle of burning its stockpile of two and a half tons of raw turtle shells that had been illegally collected for export. The burning took place in front of the world press and contestants for the 1998 Miss World Contest, and the vice president and minister of the environment lit the fire. The Seychelles, whose people hunted local sea turtles for centuries, has taken strong action in recent years to encourage conservation in order to protect its vital tourist industry from negative campaigns by turtle protection activists.

Trade continues

Despite protective legislation and global publicity, international trade in hawksbill shells does continue in some countries, and the tortoiseshell trade poses a significant threat to the survival of the hawksbill species. One proposed solution to this crisis is the farming of turtles for their shells. A turtle farm in the Cayman Islands of the Caribbean, for example, has managed to produce a green sea turtle whose shell is as beautiful as that of the hawksbill. The turtles are raised in very shallow pens so their shells are exposed to more sun than they would be in the wild, a small detail that produces shells more clearly and ornately marked than those of the ordinary green turtle.

To justify their farming practices and the slaughtering of farmed turtles for these ornate shells, the farmers contend

The sale of turtle shells continues in some countries despite international protective treaties that prohibit it.

that they are simply meeting the demand for ornate shells. They argue that their practices take pressure off the wild hawksbill populations and boost numbers because their shells are obtained from farm-raised turtles rather than from wild populations threatened with extinction.

Environmentalists are concerned, though, that to an untrained eye, it is difficult to tell the difference between the shells of the farmed green turtle and the wild hawksbill turtle. They worry that this makes it easier for wild hawksbill shells to find their way to market as "farmed" green turtle shells, and they argue that turtle farming perpetuates the demand for endangered animals, making poaching more likely.

Radio transmitters on turtle shells

Farming of green sea turtles is one possible way to prevent endangered species from becoming extinct. Another important technique to save endangered turtle species is research to better understand their life cycles, habitats, and ranges. As a result, researchers have tracked, monitored, and attached radio transmitters to the shells of endangered and threatened land turtles. The travels and habits of wood turtles and bog turtles, for instance, are being closely monitored and recorded in the hopes that this information will provide clues as to how to protect these species and preserve their limited habitats.

To obtain long-term data on the status of Florida's nesting sea turtles, for example, the Florida Department of Natural Resources and the U.S. Fish and Wildlife Service are working together to study about 190 miles of nesting beaches. Researchers attached radio transmitters to the shells of sea turtles, and the transmitters then sent signals to satellites whenever the turtles came up for air, allowing scientists to track typical migratory patterns. Using computer mapping programs, researchers can see where the turtles migrate, what routes they travel, and how fast they swim. The U.S. Army Corps of Engineers then used the signals from turtles' radio transmitters to know when turtles were absent from Tampa Bay, Florida, so that the ship-

Radio transmitters, such as the one attached to this loggerhead turtle, are used by researchers to track and monitor turtles.

ping channel could be dredged without injuring the animals.

In other parts of the world, scientists also use transmitters to show governmental authorities which turtle habitats need to be protected. Malaysia and the Philippines have, as a result, established marine national parks to protect some island beaches where green sea turtles come ashore to lay their eggs. To track the turtles when they return to the sea after laying their eggs, biologists in those countries have glued satellite transmitter tags to the shells of female turtles. The tags transmit a signal to a satellite at the U.S. National Oceanic and Atmospheric Administration, so that scientists can download data on the turtles' travels. According to Michael Stuwe of the Smithsonian Institution, "If we know how far from the beach the turtles go, we can try to influence the authorities to extend the protected area and make sure patrol boats keep trawlers out."[15]

Saving the Kemp's ridley turtle

Radio transmitters are also being used in Texas, the state that has traditionally led the nation in numbers of dead or injured sea turtles (450 sea turtles washed ashore dead in 1999, of which 95 were Kemp's ridleys), as part of a breeding program on Padre Island. Researchers attach radio transmitters to the shells of Kemp's ridley turtles in an effort to track them and record their breeding patterns. About the size of a deck of cards, each transmitter costs approximately twenty-five hundred dollars and is glued to the top of the turtle's shell.

This breeding program is based on the fact that Kemp's ridley sea turtles return in large groups to the same beaches to nest. Historically, these turtles have returned to the beaches in Rancho Nuevo, Mexico; however, in the 1970s scientists discovered a ridley nest on Padre Island. Biologists decided to try to establish a second breeding colony on the island's beaches, only a few hundred miles from the Mexican nesting site.

From 1978 to 1988, more than twenty-two thousand turtle eggs were removed from nests on the Mexican beach and buried on Padre Island. Biologists also caught thousands of young hatchlings before they returned to the sea and flew them instead to the Padre Island turtle nursery, where they were kept until they were large enough to tag and release into the Gulf of Mexico. Of the original twenty-two thousand eggs, thirteen thousand turtles hatched, grew to the size of dinner plates, and were set free in the Texas Gulf. By 1999 at least five of those tagged turtles had returned by themselves to nest on Padre Island. Although this number may seem tiny, biologists are encouraged by each individual success of the breeding program, and they hypothesize that many more tagged turtles return to nest on Gulf beaches without detection.

Small numbers of Kemp's ridley sea turtles are now nesting on Padre Island due to the efforts of scientists who researched their breeding patterns and relocated thousands of hatchlings.

The value of live turtles

Tagging and tracking sea turtles is only one aspect of an effective conservation program. Another aspect is helping change local attitudes and creating alternative income sources. The beach in the Caribbean village of Tortuguero, Costa Rica, for example, was a well-known nesting site as well as a popular turtle hunting spot. In 1975 the area was turned into a national park, and today the local economy is based not on harvesting turtles but on showing them to tourists. Since more than fifteen thousand visitors come to Tortuguero each year, turtles are worth more alive than dead. "A live animal benefits the community," says park director Eduardo Chamorro. "If you kill it, you have a meal. Alive, people come again and again to see it."[16] This strategy of increasing the local value of live turtles is gaining momentum as a way to protect endangered animals from hunting and poaching.

Dr. Peter Pritchard, head of the Chelonian Research Institute in Oviedo, Florida, has pioneered this strategy along the Atlantic coast of Guyana, where overhunting by the local Arawak Indians had seriously damaged the sea turtle population. Pritchard worked with the government to establish chicken farming as an alternative to turtle hunting, and his local research group hires Arawak people to tag turtles and defend nesting grounds. His program has encouraged the local people to become protectors of turtles, and the killing of sea turtles there has largely stopped.

A similar program in Brazil combines the release of hatchlings, promotion of turtle tourism, and reeducation of former turtle hunters. Called Tamar, this program oversees 620 miles of Brazilian coastline, employing four hundred local residents as part-time beach monitors. Each monitor watches over about 2 miles of beach, watching over turtle nests or transporting eggs to hatcheries if the nests seem to be threatened.

Tamar's success is built on ecotourism, or travel by people who want to support environmentally friendly programs with their vacation dollars. The program has built a visitors' center, which is visited by three hundred thousand

Tortuguero National Park (pictured) and other national preserves provide safe habitats for turtles.

tourists each year. Many of the tourists buy turtle souvenirs made by local residents, which helps the economy. Furthermore, the fifteen hotels that have sprung up to serve the tourist trade have been built far back from the beach, with low profiles and limited beach lighting.

Protection of turtles on land

Although efforts to conserve and protect sea turtle species receive a disproportionate amount of governmental and media attention, there are efforts to protect turtle habitats on land as well. In an attempt to protect the diverse species that rely on them, wetlands are regulated under state and federal laws such as the Clean Water Act. Citing this act, the National Wildlife Federation recently went to court to obtain the suspension of a broad permit that allowed the filling of wetlands for construction of single-family homes without public notice or environmental review. Although the case is still pending, environmentalists are hopeful for a positive outcome.

Private and public agencies are also buying up land and creating nature preserves where endangered turtles live. The Nature Conservancy, a nationwide conservation organization, has worked with private donors and public agencies to purchase thousands of wetland acres along the eastern seaboard, protecting bits of the bog turtle's remaining habitat. In 1996, for instance, one Pennsylvania county government gave $190,000 to this conservation group to expand a bog turtle site by 130 acres. Similarly, the Audubon Society estimates that its local programs have protected six hundred thousand wetland acres since 1990 by creating public and private wildlife sanctuaries and education centers.

What the future holds

Despite widespread current efforts at conservation and preservation of turtles and their habitats, scientists predict that many of the currently endangered species will become extinct in the near future. The continuing plight of the Kemp's ridley is one example. Despite more than twenty years of biologists' efforts to incubate eggs, protect hatchlings, and return juveniles to the sea, combined with conservationists' efforts to mandate turtle excluder devices (TEDs) and protect nesting beaches, the Kemp's ridley is still the rarest of all the sea turtles. Fewer than two thousand female adult Kemp's ridley turtles remain today.

Perhaps the lesson behind the unfinished story of the Kemp's ridley turtle is that saving any species of endangered turtle will require a cooperative and concerted effort by government officials, industry (whether it be fishing or manufacturing), conservationists, educators, and local citizens. Sea turtle breeding programs cannot be successful without concurrent enforcement of TED usage and no-fishing zones, and land conservation will not save terrestrial turtles without pollution prevention and well-planned suburban development. Until and unless all of these protective measures are implemented, many turtle species will continue their slow but steady slide toward extinction.

Appendix

U.S. Turtle Species Listed as Threatened or Endangered by
the U.S. Fish and Wildlife Service as of January 31, 2000

Endangered	Date first listed
Hawksbill sea turtle	1970
Kemp's ridley sea turtle	1970
Leatherback sea turtle	1970
Green sea turtle	1978
Plymouth redbelly turtle	1980
Alabama redbelly turtle	1987

Threatened	Date first listed
Loggerhead sea turtle	1978
Olive ridley sea turtle	1978
Desert tortoise	1980
Ringed map turtle	1986
Gopher tortoise	1987
Bog turtle	1997
Flattened musk turtle	1987
Yellow-blotched map turtle	1991

Notes

Introduction

1. Richard E. Nicholls, *The Running Press Book of Turtles.* Philadelphia: Running, 1977, p. 107.

Chapter 1: The Evolution and Life Cycle of Turtles

2. Quoted in Les Line, "Fast Decline of Slow Species," *National Wildlife*, October/November 1998, p. 26.

Chapter 2: Hunting and Poaching

3. Quoted in Nicholls, *The Running Press Book of Turtles,* p. 109.

4. Quoted in Molly Moore, "Mexicans Waylay Unprotected Turtles; Marines Guarding Endangered Species Shifted to Site of Rebel Attack," *Washington Post,* October 10, 1996, p. A41.

Chapter 3: Fishing and Sea Turtles

5. Quoted in Jo Warrick, "At Sea, the Catchword Is Conservation; New Rules Force Fisheries to Reduce Destructive 'Bycatch,'" *Washington Post,* January 1999, p. A1.

6. Quoted in Peter L. Lutz and John A. Musick, eds., *The Biology of Sea Turtles.* Boca Raton, FL: CRC, 1997, p. 403.

Chapter 4: Destruction of the Sea Turtle's Habitats

7. Quoted in Willie Howard, "Sargassum Harvest Should End," Palm Beach Interactive Website.www.gopbi.com/recreation/outdoors/sargassum.html.

Chapter 5: Destruction of Land and Freshwater Turtle Habitats

8. Quoted in Line, "Fast Decline of Slow Species," p. 27.

9. Rick Hampson, "Tiny Turtle Has Friends and Foes," *USA Today,* April 30, 1999, p. 3A.

10. Quoted in Hampson, "Tiny Turtle Has Friends and Foes," p. 3A.

11. Quoted in Ron Matus, "Developers, Do-Gooders Doing Harm to Tortoises," *Gainesville (Florida) Sun,* June 7, 1999, p. A1.

Chapter 6: The Law and the Future

12. *Turtle and Tortoise Newsletter,* 2000, pp. 2–3. www.chelonian.org/ttn:.

13. Office of Protected Resources, NMFS. "Endangered Species Act of 1973." www.nmfs.noaa.gov/prot_res/esa-home.html.

14. Anders G. J. Rhodin, "Publisher's Editorial: Turtle Survival Crisis," *Turtle and Tortoise Newsletter,* January 2000. www.chelonian.org/ttn/archives/ttn1/pp2-3.shtml.

15. Quoted in Sharon Begley and Erika Check, "High Tech Goes Wild," *Newsweek,* January 31, 2000, p. 57.

16. Quoted in Anne and Jack Rudloe, "Sea Turtles: In a Race for Survival," *National Geographic,* February 1994, p. 118.

Glossary

aphrodisiac: A food or drug that arouses or is thought to arouse sexual desire.

biodegradable: Something able to be broken down or dissolved by natural forces such as sun, rain, and wind.

bycatch: Marine animals that are unintentionally trapped in fishing and shrimping nets.

carapace: The top shell of a turtle, made up of a bony layer and a layer of tough scalelike scutes.

chelonian: A classification term meaning "turtle."

cotylosaurs: Lizardlike, insect-eating, and heavily limbed amphibious reptiles with solid roofed skulls and labyrinthine teeth, who lived during the age of reptiles.

DDT: A commonly used agricultural pesticide until the 1970s, when it was found to be toxic and dangerous to animals and humans.

endangered: A species rare enough to be threatened with extinction.

extinct: A species no longer in existence.

fibropapilloma: Lobe-shaped tumors appearing in rapidly increasing numbers on the bodies of sea turtles around the world. Seen on the skin, between scales and scutes, in the mouth, on the eyes, and on internal organs, the tumors can increase in size and number until a turtle is seriously debilitated.

hatchling: A very young and defenseless turtle that has just emerged from an egg.

herpetologist: A scientist who studies reptiles and amphibians.

PCBs: Short for "polychlorinated biphenyls"; poisonous chemicals used in industry and manufacturing, PCBs are toxic to all living things.

plastron: The bottom shell of a turtle, made up of a bony layer and a layer of tough scalelike scutes.

poaching: The taking of game or fish illegally.

predation: The act of killing and eating animals.

riparian: Living or located on the bank of a river, stream, or brook, or sometimes of a lake or a tidewater.

sargassum: An abundant brown algae that grows near the surface in warm waters of the western North Atlantic and floats in large rafts, traveling about with the wind and currents; also known as gulfweed.

scutes: Components of the scalelike outer layer of a turtle's shell, made of a semitransparent hornlike substance similar to the scales of a snake or lizard.

stranding: When a dead or dying sea turtle washes up on a beach.

sustainable: Something in an amount able to be supported and continued by natural forces.

terrapin: The name given to any of several species of turtle that are edible, hard-shelled, and found in coastal areas.

threatened: A species having an uncertain chance of continued survival; likely to become endangered.

tortoise: Any turtle species that lives on land.

tortoiseshell: The valuable and sought-after black and yellow shell of the hawksbill turtle, used to make decorations, utensils, and jewelry.

Organizations to Contact

Archie Carr Center for Sea Turtle Research
PO Box 118525
University of Florida
Gainesville, FL 32611
(352) 392-5194
Fax: (352) 392-9166
e-mail: accstr@zoo.ufl.edu
website: accstr.ufl.edu

The mission of the Archie Carr Center for Sea Turtle Research is to conduct research in all aspects of the biology of sea turtles, to train graduate students, and to further sea turtle conservation by communicating these research results to the scientific community, management agencies, and conservation organizations throughout the world.

California Turtle and Tortoise Club (CTTC)
Tortuga Gazette
PO Box 7300
Van Nuys, CA 91409-7300
website: www.tortoise.org/

The CTTC was founded in 1964 and has over twenty-eight hundred members worldwide. It bills itself as the most complete turtle and tortoise site on the Internet.

Center for Marine Conservation (CMC)
1725 DeSales St., NW, Suite 600
Washington, DC 20036
(202) 429-5609
Fax: (202) 872-0619

e-mail: cmc@dccmc.org
website: www.cmc-ocean.org/

The CMC specializes in helping sea turtles. It is committed to protecting ocean environments and conserving the global abundance and diversity of marine life. Through science-based advocacy, research, and public education, the CMC promotes informed citizen participation to reverse the degradation of the oceans.

Chicago Turtle Club
c/o Jan Spitzer
1939 W. Lunt
Chicago, IL 60626
website: www.geocities.com/~chicagoturtle/

The Chicago Turtle Club was founded to provide information to local turtle enthusiasts who seek more information or help in maintaining the well-being, safety, and environment of their turtles and tortoises. It offers a newsletter and regular meetings.

Desert Tortoise Preserve Committee, Inc.
4067 Mission Inn Ave.
Riverside, CA 92501
(909) 683-3872
Fax: (909) 683-6949
website: www.tortoise-tracks.org/

The Desert Tortoise Preserve Committee was formed in 1974 to promote the welfare of the desert tortoise in its native wild state. Committee activities include: establishing desert tortoise preserves; developing and implementing management programs for tortoise preserves and adjacent areas; providing education and conducting research.

Help Endangered Animals—Ridley Turtles (HEART)
PO Box 681231
Houston, TX 77268-1231
website: www.ridleyturtles.org

HEART was organized in 1982 to save the Kemp's ridley sea turtle from extinction by educating the public and supporting conservation laws that protect sea turtles. HEART serves as an educational referral source for teachers and students seeking information about the Kemp's ridleys and all sea turtles. A grassroots, all-volunteer organization, HEART strives to inform the public of breaking news about Kemp's ridleys and the challenges facing their survival.

Humane Society of the United States,
Wildlife and Habitat Protection Program
2100 L St., NW
Washington, DC 20037
(202) 452-1100
website:
www.hsus.org/programs/wildlife/seaturtles/index.html

Through its wildlife and Habitat Protection Program, the Humane Society works to control the international trade in freshwater turtles and tortoises, promotes the use of turtle excluder devices, and supports the creation of safety zones for nesting and offshore sea turtles.

Mid-Atlantic Turtle and Tortoise Society (MATTS)
2914 E. Joppa Rd., #103
Baltimore, MD 21234-3031
(410) 882-2769
Fax: (410) 882-0839
website: www.matts.herptiles.com/

MATTS is dedicated to the worldwide conservation and husbandry of turtles and tortoises.

Office of Protected Resources
National Oceanic and Atmospheric Administration
1315 East-West Hwy.
Silver Spring, Maryland 20910
(301) 713-1401
Fax: (301) 713-0376
website: www.nmfs.noaa.gov/prot_res/turtles/turtle.html

The Office of Protected Resources provides program oversight, national policy direction, and guidance on the conservation of marine mammals and endangered species and their habitats. It develops national guidelines and policies for protected resources programs and provides advice and guidance on scientific aspects of managing protected species and marine protected areas.

New York Turtle and Tortoise Society (NYTTS)
163 Amsterdam Ave., Suite 365
New York, NY 10023
(212) 459-4803
website: www.nytts.org/

The NYTTS is dedicated to education on the conservation of turtles and tortoises, the preservation of their habitat, and the promotion of proper husbandry and captive propagation.

Sea Turtle, Inc. (STI)
PO Box 3987
South Padre Island, TX 78597
(956) 761-4511

Sea Turtle, Inc., was founded in 1977 to assist in the preservation and protection of the Kemp's ridley sea turtle and to ultimately restore the ridley population to a level that will ensure its survival. Through the years STI has expanded its scope to actively support the conservation of all marine turtle species. To achieve its goals, STI provides educational programs to schools, tourist bureaus, civic organizations and news media. STI also assists and supports the U.S. Department of the Interior with its efforts to establish a nesting beach for the Kemp's ridley on North Padre Island.

Sea Turtle Restoration Project (STRP)
PO Box 400
Forest Knolls, CA 94933
(415) 488-0370
Fax: (415) 488-0372
website: http://seaturtles.org

The STRP works to protect sea turtle populations in ways that meet the ecological needs of the sea turtles as well as the needs of the local communities that share the beaches and waters with these endangered species.

Sea Turtle Survival League
4424 NW 13th St., Suite A1
Gainesville, FL 32609
(352) 373-6441
website: www.cccturtle.org/

The nonprofit Sea Turtle Survival League is dedicated to protecting endangered and threatened sea turtles through research, education, and advocacy.

Turtle Time, Inc.
PO Box 2621
Fort Myers Beach, FL 33932
(941) 481-5566
website: www.swflorida.com/turtletime/

Turtle Time, Inc., is a not-for-profit organization dedicated to the continued survival of loggerhead sea turtles. Established in 1989, the group is Florida's monitoring organization for sea turtle activity from Fort Myers Beach to the Lee-Collier County line. Daily patrols during the nesting season are conducted to gather important scientific data about population estimates, distribution of nests, nesting patterns, and hatching success rates.

Wildlife Conservation Society
Turtle Recovery Program
2300 Southern Blvd.
Bronx, NY 10460
website: www.wcs.org/mainmenu.html

Through its Turtle Recovery Program, the Wildlife Conservation Society sponsors scientific studies and plans conservation programs to help turtles and tortoises all over the world.

Suggestions for Further Reading

Books

Virginia Alvin and Robert Silverstein, *Saving Endangered Animals*. Hillside, NJ: Enslow, 1993. Discusses the endangerment and extinction of different species of wildlife and the conservation efforts now under way.

Anita Baskin-Salzberg and Allen Salzberg, *Turtles*. New York: Franklin Watts, 1996. A thorough, general introduction to all of the different types of turtles and how they are being threatened today, with beautiful photos throughout.

Carl H. Ernst, Jeffrey E. Lovich, and Roger W. Barbour, *Turtles of the United States and Canada*. Washington, DC: Smithsonian Institution, 1994. Includes thorough descriptions and photos of each of the fifty-six species of turtles found in the United States and Canada, along with sections on anatomy, geographic distribution, and habitat and a key to identifying the different species.

Liz Palika, *The Complete Idiot's Guide to Turtles and Tortoises*. New York: MacMillan, 1998. Contains information on every aspect of turtle care, presented in an accessible, quick, fun format, with care tips, pitfalls, and interesting trivia bits throughout.

Noel Simon, *Nature in Danger: Threatened Habitats and Species*. New York: Oxford University Press, 1995. Examines the flora and fauna of different endangered ecosystems, discusses human effects on these areas, and highlights various endangered species and what is being done to preserve them.

Hartmut Wilke and M. Heimter, *Turtles and Tortoises: Caring for Them, Feeding Them, Understanding Them.* Hauppauge, NY: Barron's Educational Series, 1998. Offers practical advice on the care of tortoises, geared to families and children who have little or no experience taking care of pets.

Websites

HerpMed's Turtle Website
(www.xmission.com/~gastown/herpmed/chelonia.htm). Contains a long list of website links.

National Audubon Society, Wetlands Campaign
(www.audubon.org/campaign/wetland/). This site chronicles the local and regional programs that have preserved six hundred thousand acres of wetlands since 1990.

Turtle Trax (www.turtles.org). This website was created to help people become familiar with sea turtles, especially the Hawaiian green turtle.

U.S. Fish and Wildlife Endangered Species Program
(http://endangered.fws.gov/endspp.html). This website lists currently endangered and threatened species and many articles and press releases on the current status of a variety of species.

Wilderness Society (http://wilderness.org/). This site lists the organization's current campaigns to protect habitats of threatened and endangered species in several parts of the country.

Works Consulted

Books

David Alderton, *Turtles and Tortoises of the World*. New York: Facts On File, 1988. Contains a comprehensive description of turtle biology, a summary of turtle evolution, a lengthy list of sample species, and some older information on the interaction between turtles and humans.

Karen A. Bjorndal, ed., *Biology and Conservation of Sea Turtles*. Washington, DC: Smithsonian Institution, 1995. Discusses the basic biology of sea turtles, the status of sea turtle populations, and conservation theory, techniques, problems, and law.

Philippe De Vosjoli, *General Care and Maintenance of Popular Tortoises*. Lakeside, CA: Advanced Vivarian Systems, 1997. Covers care and husbandry of the most popular and common turtles, including information on selection, housing design and landscaping, feeding and watering, diseases and disorders, hygiene, and more.

Carl H. Ernst and Roger W. Barbour, *Turtles of the World*. Washington, DC: Smithsonian Institution, 1994. An extremely comprehensive and technical listing of all of the world's turtle species, with photographs. Each entry includes how to recognize the species and its distribution, habitat, and natural history.

Peter L. Lutz and John A. Musick, eds., *The Biology of Sea Turtles*. Boca Raton, FL: CRC, 1997. A compilation of scholarly research, this book focuses on how sea turtles operate in and are dependent on specific characteristics of their marine environment.

Anthony V. Margavio, et al., *Caught in the Net: The Conflict Between Shrimpers and Conservationists.* College Station: Texas A&M University Press, 1996. Tells the story of conflicts between shrimpers and environmentalists trying to protect turtles from being caught in shrimp nets. Draws on interviews with shrimpers, policymakers, researchers, and others connected with the shrimping industry.

Richard E. Nicholls, *The Running Press Book of Turtles.* Philadelphia: Running, 1977. This author's premise is that, because turtles have existed for so long and through such great climate changes and disruptions, we can learn from their remarkable adaptability. He suggests that turtles will only continue to survive if humans change their actions.

Periodicals

Sharon Begley and Erika Check, "High Tech Goes Wild," *Newsweek,* January 31, 2000.

Larry Bingham, "Mom Is Alive! And Other Interesting Facts About Endangered Sea Turtles," *Fort Worth Star-Telegram,* January 23, 1999.

———, "A Year of Living Dangerously; Biologists Track Endangered Sea Turtles as They Make a Perilous Annual Swim Across the Gulf of Mexico," *Fort Worth Star-Telegram,* October 14, 1998.

Jane Bussey, "Panel Says Dwindling Sea Turtles Need Help; But U.S. Laws May Delay Plan," *Miami Herald,* April 9, 1999.

L. Carie, "Turtles Reduce Shrimp Harvest," *Daytona Beach News-Journal,* May 14, 1999.

Carol B. Cole, "Turtles Don't Yield; Eggs Laid in Zone Set Aside for Vehicles," *Daytona Beach News-Journal,* May 30, 1997.

Katherine Ellison, "Saving the Sea Turtles in Brazil; Ecology: Conservationists Have Made Tourism the

Keystone of a Project Dedicated to Protecting Endangered Species," *Baltimore Sun,* November 23, 1998.

Brian Feagans, "Visiting Turtles Prompt Change in Shrimper Nets," *Wilmington (North Carolina) Morning Star-News,* June 2, 1999.

Jim Graham, "Sell a Turtle, Risk a Poaching Charge; New Regulations Protect Four Native New Hampshire Species from Being Caught and Sold," *Concord (New Hampshire) Monitor,* June 2, 1996.

Ted Gregory, "Nowhere to Hide? In Dwindling Wetlands, Researcher on Lookout for Blanding's Turtles," *Chicago Tribune,* August 1, 1994.

Rick Hampson, "Tiny Turtle Has Friends and Foes," *USA Today,* April 30, 1999.

Lynne Langley, "Sargassum Loss Threatens Fish," *Charleston Post and Courier,* November 22, 1998.

David Aquila Lawrence, "Globe-Girdling Sea Turtles Start to Get Global Protection; U.S. Enforced Its Own Law this Month as an American Treaty Moved Toward Ratification," *Christian Science Monitor,* May 18, 1999.

Les Line, "Fast Decline of Slow Species," *National Wildlife,* October/November 1998.

John MacCormick, "Officials Struggle to Identify What's Killing Kemp's Ridleys," *San Antonio Express-News,* April 14, 1998.

Ron Matus, "Developers, Do-Gooders Doing Harm to Tortoises," *Gainesville (Florida) Sun,* June 7, 1999.

———, "Poaching Still Alive in Florida," *Gainesville (Florida) Sun,* July 5, 1998.

Molly Moore, "Mexicans Waylay Unprotected Turtles; Marines Guarding Endangered Species Shifted to Site of Rebel Attack," *Washington Post,* October 10, 1996.

Tim Padgett, "Peter Pritchard: Tickled About Turtles," *Time,* February 28, 2000.

James Pinkerton, "Sea Turtles from Both Sides of Net," *Houston Chronicle,* December 20, 1998.

Craig Pittman, "Technology Tails Turtles," *St. Petersburg (Florida) Times,* September 6, 1998.

Anne and Jack Rudloe, "Sea Turtles: In a Race for Survival," *National Geographic,* February 1994.

Dave Smith, "Turtles Basking on Isle Shores Confound Scientists," *Hawaii Tribune-Herald,* February 28, 1999.

Tony Vindell, "Shrimpers Help with Turtle Rescue Program; Dedication of New Camp Set for Today," *Brownsville (Texas) Herald,* May 31, 1998.

Jo Warrick, "At Sea, the Catchword Is Conservation; New Rules Force Fisheries to Reduce Destructive 'Bycatch,'" *Washington Post,* January 1999.

Tim Wheeler and Dennis O'Brien, "Bog Turtle Is a Threatened Species; Reptile's Habitat Is Being Destroyed," *Baltimore Sun,* November 5, 1997.

Bernice C. Wuethrich, "Into Dangerous Waters," *International Wildlife Magazine,* March/April 1996.

Pamphlets

Florida Power and Light, "Sea Turtles and Lights," 1993.

Peter Fugazzotto and Chitta Behera, "Dead Turtles: Good for the Global Economy?" Sea Turtle Restoration Project and Project Swarajya, November 1999.

Victoria B. Van Meter, "Florida's Sea Turtles," Department of Environmental Protection, Office of Protected Species Management, Florida Power and Light, 1992.

Internet Sources

Willie Howard, "Sargassum Harvest Should End," Palm Beach Interactive Website. www.gopbi.com/recreation/outdoors/sargassum.html.

Anders G. J. Rhodin, "Publisher's Editorial: Turtle Survival Crisis," *Turtle and Tortoise Newsletter,* January 2000. www.chelonian.org/ttn/archives/ttn1/pp2-3.shtml.

Turtle Time, "Turtle Friendly Tips: Facts About Sea Turtles." http://swflorida.com/turtletime/index_frame.htm.

Wildlife Conservation Society. "Turtle Workshop Recommendations and Conclusions." www.wcs.org/search/.

Index

Picture Credits

About the Author

Joan C. Hawxhurst is the author of a number of books for children and young adults, on topics as varied as the Second Amendment, Mother Jones, and interfaith families. She has lived in Argentina, Haiti, and France, as well as Colorado, Maryland, and New York. She currently lives in the woods outside Kalamazoo, Michigan, with her husband, two children, a cat, and a dog. This is her first book on animals.